Acknowledgments

With deep gratitude, I present " Interview Alchemy":

Transforming Opportunities into Offers. To my mentors, your

unwavering support, wisdom, and guidance shaped this book. To

all mentors, your teachings empower countless readers. This book

is a collective effort, a testament to professional connections. …

About the Author

Nithin Hassan is a pioneer in the

tech industry with over two

decades of experience, making

significant strides not only in his

field but also in the realm of career

coaching. A beacon for aspiring

professionals, Nithin's deep-rooted

knowledge of software and his

commitment to guiding job seekers have propelled many to

impressive career heights. His tenure at leading companies, including Meta, Microsoft, and Amazon Web Services, has equipped him with unparalleled insights into the hiring process. This expertise has been pivotal in mentoring individuals to achieve their career aspirations, shaping interviewees into confident, standout candidates ready to seize their ideal job opportunities. Marked by significant achievements, such as spearheading major data center initiatives and innovative cost-saving solutions, Nithin's greatest fulfillment comes from fostering career growth in others. As a mentor and coach, he has inspired numerous professionals along their journey to success. His book, "Interview Alchemy," encapsulates Nithin's dedication to empowering job seekers. It compiles his extensive wisdom into an essential guide for acing interviews, providing the necessary tools and tactics for candidates at every level. Beyond his book, Nithin continues to enrich the professional community through his CareerKickstartClub.com.

Table of Contents

Chapter 1: The Art of Interviewing

Embark on your journey by delving into the essence of interviews. In this Chapter, you will explore why interviews become a vital part of your career path and set the stage for mastering them.

1.1 Understanding the Interview Landscape

- **Identify Your Potential Interviews**: Start by evaluating the types of interviews commonly associated with your field and career level. Research the industry norms and speak to professionals with experience in your desired field to gain insights into the prevalent interview formats.

- **Prepare for Each Interview Type**: Once you've identified the potential interview formats, tailor your preparation accordingly. For instance, if you anticipate behavioral interviews, practice responding to behavioral questions using the STAR (Situation, Task, Action, Result) method. If technical interviews are common, brush up on technical concepts and problem-solving skills.

- **Consider Your Career Level**: Different career levels may require different types of interviews. For entry-level positions, you might encounter more traditional interviews focusing on your qualifications and soft skills. Higher-level positions may involve panel interviews or case interviews. Understand where you stand in your career and prepare accordingly.

- **Know the Purpose**: Recognize that interviews are crucial for employers to evaluate your qualifications, skills, and cultural fit. Approach each interview with the mindset that it's an opportunity for you and the employer to determine if the partnership is a mutual fit.

- **Assess Cultural Alignment**: Understand that interviews are not just about your qualifications; they also gauge your alignment with the company's culture and values. Research the organization's culture beforehand and be prepared to discuss how your values align with theirs during the interview.

• **Prepare Questions**: Tailor your questions for the interview based on their type and purpose. Consider asking about the team's technical challenges if it's a technical interview. For a cultural fit interview, inquire about the company's values and mission. Show your genuine interest in the role by asking insightful questions.

• **Practice Versatility**: Be adaptable in your interview approach. Even if you expect a particular interview type, be ready to pivot if the conversation takes a different direction. Versatility demonstrates your ability to think on your feet and handle unexpected situations.

• **Reflect and Learn**: Reflect on your performance and the interview type after each interview. Consider what went well and what you could improve. Use this feedback to refine your preparation for future interviews of the same or different types.

- **Seek Guidance**: If you need more clarification about the types of interviews you may face or need guidance on preparing for specific formats, seek advice from mentors, career coaches, or professionals with experience in your target field.

By proactively understanding the various interview types and their purposes, you can tailor your interview strategy and preparation to maximize your chances of success. Each interview format offers unique opportunities to showcase your qualifications and fit for the role, and being well-prepared for each type is a crucial step toward interview excellence.

1.2 The Role of Interviews in Your Career Journey

Interviews are not merely stepping stones in your professional path; they are the bridges that connect your aspirations to reality. This chapter unravels the profound role interviews play in shaping your career journey.

Pivotal Milestones: Interviews are more than just meetings; they are key moments that can redefine your career trajectory. Each interview is a unique opportunity that can open doors to new roles, promotions, and significant leaps forward in your professional life.

The Gateway to Opportunities: Interviews are the gateways through which you enter new chapters of your career story. They allow you to demonstrate your skills, knowledge, and potential to prospective employers, paving the way for exciting opportunities and growth.

A Positive Professional Reputation: The way you handle interviews speaks volumes about your professionalism and competence. Consistent success in interviews not only leads to job offers but also contributes to building a positive professional reputation in your industry.

Continuous Growth and Development: Interviews are not just about landing a job but also opportunities for self-discovery and improvement. Whether successful or not, each interview offers lessons that contribute to your personal and professional development.

In this chapter, you'll gain a deep appreciation for the role of interviews in your career journey. You'll discover how interviews are not isolated events but integral to your ongoing growth and success. As you embark on your journey to master the art of interviews, remember that every interview is a step toward achieving your career goals.

Chapter 2: Preparing for Interview Success

In this chapter, you will discover how to lay the foundation for success. Craft a powerful resume and cover letter, ensuring you make a standout first impression in a competitive job market.

2.1 Crafting Your Personal Brand

In the competitive landscape of job interviews, your personal brand is your unique selling proposition. This chapter explores how you can strategically craft and present your personal brand to stand out in any interview scenario.

Understanding Personal Branding: Your personal brand reflects your professional identity. It encompasses your skills, experiences, values, and the image you project to potential employers. Discover the power of personal branding and how it can differentiate you from other candidates.

Tailoring Your Brand to the Job: One size doesn't fit all in personal branding. Learn how to customize your brand to align with the specific job you're interviewing for. Whether it's highlighting your leadership skills, technical expertise, or problem-solving abilities, your personal brand should resonate with the role.

2.2 Resume Magic: Making Your First Impression Count

By mastering the art of resume writing, you'll craft a document that not only secures your place in the interview queue but also positions you as a top candidate. Your resume becomes your advocate, making your first impression count and unlocking doors to exciting career opportunities.

Creating a resume that stands out is crucial in today's competitive job market. Here's a step-by-step guide to help you craft an outstanding resume:

1. Understand the Purpose:

- Before you start, it's essential to grasp the purpose of your resume: to secure an interview. Keep this in mind throughout the process.

2. Choose the Right Format:

- Resume formats include chronological, functional, and combination/hybrid. Choose one that best highlights your qualifications. For example, a chronological resume is suitable if you have a strong work history.

Sample Resume Content:

[Your Name]

[Your Phone Number] | [Your Email Address] | [LinkedIn Profile]

Objective:

[Brief summary of your career goals and qualifications.]

Education:

[Degree, Major] | [University Name] | [Graduation Date]

Work Experience:

[Job Title] | [Company Name] | [Dates of Employment]

- [List of responsibilities and achievements using action verbs and metrics.]

3. Contact Information:

- Include your name, phone number, professional email address, and a link to your LinkedIn profile (if applicable). Ensure your email address is professional, e.g., firstname.lastname@email.com.

4. Create Clear Headings:

- Organize your resume with clear headings to make it easy to navigate. Common sections include:

- Contact Information

- Objective or Summary

- Education

- Work Experience

- Skills

- Certifications

- Awards and Achievements

- Additional Sections (e.g., Publications, Languages)

5. Craft a Captivating Summary or Objective:

- Write a compelling summary or objective statement that highlights your skills and goals, tailored to the job you're applying for.

Objective:

A motivated [your profession] with [X years] of experience in [key skills], seeking an opportunity to contribute my expertise to [company name] in the role of [desired job title]

6. Showcase Achievements:

- In the Work Experience section, focus on quantifiable achievements. Use action verbs and specific metrics to emphasize your contributions.

Sample Resume Content:

Work Experience:

[Job Title] | [Company Name] | [Dates of Employment]

- Increased [specific metric] by [percentage] through [action].

- Led a team of [number] members, resulting in [positive outcome].

7. Tailor to the Job:

- Customize your resume for each application. Highlight qualifications and experiences that align with the specific job requirements. Use keywords from the job description.

8. Use Action Verbs:

• Start bullet points with strong action verbs to describe your accomplishments. Action verbs convey a sense of leadership and achievement.

9. Highlight Relevant Skills:

• Include a skills section with both hard and soft skills relevant to the job. Be truthful and concise.

Sample Resume Content:

Skills:

- Technical Skills: [List relevant technical skills, e.g., programming languages, software]

- Soft Skills: [List soft skills, e.g., communication, leadership]

10. Maintain Professional Formatting: - Maintain a professional and consistent formatting style throughout your resume. Use a readable font, appropriate margins, and bullet points for easy readability.

Sample Resume Content:

[Use a clean and easy-to-read font, e.g., Arial or Calibri]

[Set appropriate margins, e.g., 1-inch]

- Use bullet points to list achievements for better readability.

11. Proofread and Edit: - Carefully proofread your resume for spelling and grammatical errors. Consider seeking feedback from peers or mentors. An error-free resume demonstrates attention to detail.

- Proofread your resume multiple times to catch any errors.

- Consider using online grammar-checking tools.

12. Quantify Achievements: - Whenever possible, use specific numbers and data to quantify your achievements.

13. Seek Professional Guidance: - If you're unsure about your resume's content, format, or overall presentation, consider consulting with a professional resume writer or career coach. They can provide valuable insights and recommendations.

14. Update Regularly: - Keep your resume up-to-date with your latest experiences, skills, and accomplishments.

15. Review and Fine-Tune: - Before submitting your resume, review it one last time to ensure it aligns with the job you're applying for and effectively communicates your qualifications.

Sample resume template.

[Your Name]

[Your Phone Number] | [Your Email Address] | [LinkedIn Profile]

Objective:

Motivated [Your Profession] with [X years] of experience in [Key Skills], seeking an opportunity to contribute my expertise to [Company Name] in the role of [Desired Job Title].

Education:

[Degree, Major]

[University Name]

[Graduation Date]

Work Experience:

[Job Title] | [Company Name] | [Dates of Employment]

- Increased [Specific Metric] by [Percentage] through [Action].

- Led a team of [Number] members, resulting in [Positive Outcome].

[Job Title] | [Company Name] | [Dates of Employment]

- Achieved [Specific Accomplishment] by [Action].

- Collaborated with [Team/Department] to [Outcome].

Skills:

- Technical Skills:

  - [List Relevant Technical Skills, e.g., Programming Languages, Software]

- Soft Skills:

  - [List Soft Skills, e.g., Communication, Leadership]

Certifications:

- [Certification Name] | [Issuing Authority] | [Date]

Awards and Achievements:

- [Award/Achievement Name] | [Year]

- [Award/Achievement Name] | [Year]

Additional Sections:

- Publications

   - [List Any Published Works or Contributions]

- Languages

   - [List Languages and Proficiency Levels]

Contact Information:

[Your Name]

[Your Phone Number]

[Your Email Address]

[LinkedIn Profile URL]

2.3 The Cover Letter Advantage

In the realm of job applications, the cover letter is your secret weapon. It's the unsung hero of your application packet, often overshadowed by the resume but possessing the potential to set you apart from the competition in profound ways.

A cover letter is a personalized introduction to you as a candidate. It offers you a valuable opportunity to communicate directly with the hiring manager or recruiter, showcasing your enthusiasm, personality, and unique qualifications. Unlike the resume, which primarily focuses on your professional background, the cover letter lets you tell your story and connect on a more human level.

Key Benefits of a Well-Crafted Cover Letter:

- **Demonstrates Genuine Interest:** Your cover letter allows you to express why you're genuinely excited about the job and the company. This demonstrates your proactive approach and genuine interest in the role.

- **Highlights Fit and Alignment:** You can use the cover letter to explain why you're an ideal fit for the position. You can draw connections between your skills, experiences, and the specific requirements of the job.

- **Personality and Culture Fit:** Employers aren't just looking for qualifications; they want to know if you'll mesh well with their team and company culture. Your cover letter can convey your personality and how you'd be a positive addition to their workplace.

- **Addresses Potential Concerns:** If you have gaps in your resume, are changing careers, or have other non-standard aspects to your application, the cover letter is the place to address these concerns honestly and positively.

- **Demonstrates Communication Skills:** A well-written cover letter is a sample of your communication abilities, a crucial skill in most jobs.

Key Elements of an Effective Cover Letter:

- **Personalization:** Address the hiring manager by name if possible. Tailor the letter to the specific job and company.

- **Clear Structure:** Follow a clear structure, including an introduction, body paragraphs, and a conclusion.

- **Engaging Opening:** Start with a compelling opening that grabs the reader's attention.

- **Storytelling:** Use examples and anecdotes to illustrate your qualifications and experiences.

- **Alignment:** Clearly connect your skills and experiences with the job requirements.

- **Enthusiasm:** Express genuine enthusiasm for the role and the company.

- **Professional Tone:** Maintain a professional and respectful tone throughout the letter.

- **Call to Action:** End the letter with a call to action, indicating your eagerness to discuss your candidacy further.

In summary, your cover letter is your chance to add depth and personality to your job application. It's an opportunity to demonstrate your genuine interest, alignment with the role, and excellent communication skills. Don't underestimate the power of a well-crafted cover letter in setting you apart from other applicants and securing that coveted interview.

Sample cover letter:

[Your Name]

[Your Address]

[City, State, ZIP Code]

[Your Email Address]

[Today's Date]

[Employer's Name]

[Company Name]

[Company Address]

[City, State, ZIP Code]

Dear [Employer's Name],

I am writing to express my enthusiastic interest in the [Job Title] position at [Company Name], as advertised on [Job Board/Company Website]. With a deep passion for [Relevant Industry/Field] and a strong commitment to excellence, I am excited about the opportunity to contribute to your dynamic team.

In my previous role at [Previous Company], I had the privilege of [Briefly Describe an Achievement or Responsibility Relevant to the Job]. This experience allowed me to [Highlight a Skill or Quality Relevant to the Job], and I am eager to leverage these skills to drive success at [Company Name].

What sets me apart as a candidate is not only my [Relevant Skill 1] and [Relevant Skill 2] but also my genuine enthusiasm for [Specific Company's Mission or Values]. Your dedication to [Specific Company's Mission or Values] resonates with me deeply, and I am excited about the prospect of contributing to your ongoing success.

Furthermore, I am impressed by [Specific Company's Recent Achievement or Initiative], which demonstrates your commitment to [Relevant Company Aspect]. I am eager to be a part of this innovative and forward-thinking environment.

Enclosed is my resume, which provides further details about my qualifications. I am excited about the opportunity to discuss how my background and experiences align with the needs of [Company Name]. Please feel free to contact me at [Your Phone Number] or [Your Email Address] to schedule a conversation.

Thank you for considering my application. I look forward to the possibility of joining your team and contributing to the continued growth and success of [Company Name].

Sincerely,

[Your Name]

2.4 Social Media Presence: A Digital Window to Your Professional World

In today's interconnected world, your social media presence plays a significant role in shaping your professional image. Potential employers, hiring managers, and recruiters often turn to platforms like LinkedIn, Twitter, and even Facebook to gain insights into your character, interests, and suitability for a job. Your social media presence can either enhance your professional reputation or raise red flags, making it crucial to curate a positive and authentic online persona.

Actions to Take for an Effective Social Media Presence:

- **Optimize Your LinkedIn Profile:** LinkedIn is the go-to platform for professional networking. Ensure your profile is complete and up-to-date, highlighting your work experience, skills, and accomplishments. Use a professional profile picture and craft a compelling headline and summary.

- **Consistency Across Platforms:** Maintain a consistent online identity across all your social media profiles. Use the same professional photo and handle (if possible) to create a unified personal brand.

- **Privacy Settings:** Review and adjust privacy settings on platforms like Facebook and Instagram to control who can see your personal content. Keep your personal life separate from your professional persona.

- **Content Sharing:** Share industry-relevant articles, insights, and your own thought leadership on platforms like

LinkedIn and Twitter. This showcases your expertise and keeps your network engaged.

- **Engagement:** Interact with others in your industry by commenting on posts, joining relevant groups, and connecting with professionals who share your interests. Engaging in conversations demonstrates your commitment to your field.

- **Showcase Your Work:** If applicable, share projects, articles, or portfolio pieces that highlight your skills and accomplishments. Visual content, such as infographics or videos, can also grab attention.

- **Professionalism:** Maintain a professional tone in your posts and interactions. Avoid controversial or offensive topics, and be mindful of your language and grammar.

- **Brand Yourself:** Use your social media presence to build a personal brand. Identify a niche or area of expertise and consistently share content related to it. This helps you stand out in your field.

- **Recommendations and Endorsements:** Request recommendations from colleagues and supervisors on LinkedIn. These endorsements add credibility to your profile.

- **Online Learning**: Share your commitment to professional growth by mentioning online courses, certifications, or webinars you've attended or completed.

- **Update Regularly:** Keep your profiles current with your latest experiences, skills, and achievements. An outdated profile may give the impression that you're not actively engaged in your field.

- **Google Yourself:** Periodically search for your own name on search engines to see what information is publicly available about you. Address any inaccuracies or negative content if necessary.

- **Clean Up Your Past:** If you have old, unprofessional content or posts on your profiles, consider removing or updating them. Your social media history can be a reflection of your growth and maturity.

Remember that your social media presence is a dynamic aspect of your professional identity. By proactively managing it, you can present a positive and authentic image to potential employers and network effectively within your industry.

Chapter 3: The Research Phase

In this chapter, you will Dive deep into research to Uncover the company culture, dissect job descriptions, and customize your interview strategy, laying the groundwork for your effective preparation.

3.1 Unveiling the Company Culture

Research is the foundation of a successful job interview. Understanding the company culture is a crucial aspect of this phase. By delving into the company's values, mission, and work environment, you can align your interview strategy and responses with what the organization is looking for in a candidate. Here, we explore how to uncover and leverage insights into the company's culture to enhance your interview preparedness.

Actions to Take for Unveiling the Company Culture:

- **Company Website Exploration:** Start with the company's official website. Look for sections like "About Us," "Mission and Values," and "Company Culture." These pages often provide an overview of the company's identity and what it values in its employees.

- **Employee Reviews**: Websites like Glassdoor, Indeed, and LinkedIn feature employee reviews and ratings. Read these to gain firsthand insights into the company's work culture, management style, and employee experiences.

- **Connect with Current or Former Employees:** Use your professional network to connect with individuals who work or have worked at the company. Reach out for informational interviews to understand their perspectives on the company's culture.

- **Social Media Analysis:** Examine the company's social media profiles, including LinkedIn, Twitter, Facebook, and Instagram. Pay attention to the type of content they share, employee testimonials, and community engagement.

- **News and Press Releases:** Search for recent news articles and press releases related to the company. This can provide information about recent achievements, strategic directions, and any noteworthy company culture initiatives.

- **LinkedIn Company Page:** Follow the company on LinkedIn and explore its company page. Look for updates, posts, and articles that shed light on their values and achievements.

- **Networking Events**: Attend industry-related events or webinars where company representatives may speak. This can offer a chance to gauge their values and corporate philosophies through their presentations and interactions.

- **Professional Groups:** Join online forums or professional groups related to your industry or the company's field. Engage in discussions and ask for opinions about the company's culture from professionals in your field.

• **Interviewer Insights:** During the interview, ask the interviewer about the company's culture, team dynamics, and what qualities they value in employees. This demonstrates your interest in fitting seamlessly into their work environment.

• **Company Culture Fit:** Reflect on your own values and work preferences. Consider whether the company's culture aligns with your personal and professional aspirations. Identifying compatibility early can save you from pursuing a job that may not be the right fit.

• **Prepare Culture-Driven Questions:** Craft questions for your interviewer that reflect your research on the company's culture. For example, you might inquire about team collaboration, diversity and inclusion initiatives, or opportunities for professional development.

- **Adapt Your Interview Strategy**: Tailor your responses to demonstrate how your values and work style align with the company's culture. Use specific examples from your experiences to showcase your compatibility.

Understanding and embracing a company's culture can significantly impact your success in the interview process. It allows you to present yourself as not only a qualified candidate but also a potential cultural fit, increasing your chances of securing a job that aligns with your career goals and values.

3.2 Understanding the Job Description

Understanding the job description is a pivotal step in preparing for a successful interview. It provides you with essential insights into what the employer is seeking in a candidate and guides your interview strategy. In this chapter, we explore how to dissect a job description effectively and tailor your approach to match the role's requirements.

Actions to Take for Understanding the Job Description:

- **Read Thoroughly:** Begin by reading the job description meticulously. Pay attention to every detail, from the job title and responsibilities to the qualifications and skills required.

- **Highlight Key Phrases:** Use a highlighter or note-taking app to mark key phrases, keywords, and specific requirements mentioned in the job description. These are crucial for tailoring your resume and interview responses.

- **Identify Core Responsibilities:** Summarize the core responsibilities of the role. Understand what the day-to-day tasks entail and envision yourself performing them.

- **Requirements Analysis:** Break down the qualifications and requirements into categories like education, experience, technical skills, and soft skills. Note whether they are "must-have" or "nice-to-have" qualifications.

• **Competency Alignment:** Evaluate how your qualifications and experiences align with the job requirements. Identify areas where you excel and others where you may need to address gaps.

• **Company Research:** Research the company's background and industry to gain a deeper understanding of how the job fits into the organization's overall goals and strategies.

• **Industry-Specific Knowledge:** If the job description mentions industry-specific knowledge or certifications, assess your proficiency in those areas and plan how to showcase them.

• **Quantify Achievements:** Prepare examples from your past experiences that demonstrate your ability to meet or exceed the job's requirements. Quantify achievements whenever possible to showcase your impact.

• **Tailor Your Resume:** Customize your resume to align with the job description. Use the highlighted keywords and phrases to emphasize your qualifications in your resume's skills and experience sections.

- **Prepare STAR Stories:** For behavioral interview questions, create Situation, Task, Action, and Result (STAR) stories that align with the job requirements. These stories illustrate how you've successfully handled similar situations in the past.

- **Ask Clarifying Questions:** If there are elements of the job description that are unclear, don't hesitate to ask the interviewer for clarification during the interview. This demonstrates your interest in the role and commitment to understanding it.

- **Professional References:** If the job description requests professional references, inform your references about the role and its requirements in advance.

- **Prepare Questions:** Craft thoughtful questions for the interviewer that reflect your understanding of the job description. Inquire about team dynamics, project expectations, or any unique challenges associated with the role.

- **Create a Job-Specific Elevator Pitch:** Develop a concise elevator pitch that highlights how your skills and experiences align with the job requirements. This can be a powerful introduction during the interview.

- **Align Your Personal Brand:** Ensure that your personal brand, as presented in your resume, cover letter, and interview, aligns seamlessly with the job description and the company's values.

Understanding the job description inside and out not only prepares you to answer interview questions effectively but also positions you as a candidate who is genuinely interested in and qualified for the role. By taking these proactive steps, you'll enhance your interview performance and increase your chances of securing your desired job.

3.3 Customizing Your Interview Strategy

In the competitive landscape of job interviews, one size does not fit all. Each job opportunity is unique, and so should your interview strategy. In this chapter, we dive into the art of customizing your interview approach to ensure you stand out as the ideal candidate for the specific role you're pursuing.

Actions to Take for Customizing Your Interview Strategy:

- **Job Description Alignment:** Revisit the job description and match it to your qualifications and experiences. Identify the key skills and requirements that the employer is seeking.

- **Highlight Relevant Experiences:** Select experiences from your professional journey that closely relate to the job's responsibilities. Tailor your resume and interview responses to emphasize these relevant experiences.

- **Industry Insights:** If the role is within a specific industry, research industry trends, challenges, and innovations. Demonstrating industry knowledge can set you apart.

- **Company Culture Fit:** Investigate the company culture by reading employee reviews, visiting the company's website and social media profiles, and networking with current or former employees.

- **Competitor Analysis:** If applicable, research the company's competitors to gain a broader understanding of the industry landscape. Knowing how the company stacks up can be insightful.

- **Prepare Role-Specific Questions:** Develop questions that directly relate to the role. These questions not only demonstrate your genuine interest but also help you gather valuable insights.

- **Cultural and Values Alignment:** Ensure that your values align with those of the company. Discuss how your personal values make you a strong cultural fit during the interview.

- **Customized Elevator Pitch:** Tailor your elevator pitch to focus on the skills and experiences most relevant to the role. Highlight what sets you apart for this particular job.

- **Addressing Weaknesses:** Be prepared to address any gaps or weaknesses in your qualifications. Discuss how you plan to overcome these challenges and contribute effectively.

- **Storytelling Approach:** Craft stories and examples that specifically align with the role's requirements. Use the STAR (Situation, Task, Action, Result) method to showcase your achievements.

- **Technical and Soft Skills:** Emphasize the technical and soft skills that are crucial for the role. Provide concrete examples of how you've applied these skills in your previous work.

- **Company-Specific Knowledge:** Familiarize yourself with the company's products, services, recent news, and achievements. Mentioning these in the interview demonstrates your commitment.

- **Personalize Your Thank-You Note:** After the interview, send a personalized thank-you note that references specific points discussed during the interview. This reinforces your interest and attentiveness.

- **LinkedIn Profile Alignment:** Ensure that your LinkedIn profile aligns with the role and industry you're targeting. Update your headline, summary, and skills to match.

- **Mock Interviews:** Conduct mock interviews tailored to the job's requirements. Seek feedback from mentors, colleagues, or professional interview coaches.

Customizing your interview strategy showcases your dedication to the role and your ability to adapt to the company's needs. By aligning your qualifications, experiences, and responses with the specific job, you increase your chances of making a memorable impression and securing your dream job.

Steps to Build a Targeted Questions List:

- **Research the Company:** Begin by thoroughly researching the company you are interviewing with. Explore its website, mission statement, values, products or services, recent news, and any publicly available financial reports. Gain a deep understanding of the company's history, culture, and industry position.

- **Analyze the Job Description:** Carefully review the job description provided by the employer. Pay attention to the qualifications, responsibilities, and skills required for the role. Identify key keywords and phrases that are repeated or emphasized.

- **Understand the Role**: Develop a comprehensive understanding of the role you are applying for. Consider the day-to-day tasks, goals, and challenges you may encounter in the position. Think about how your skills and experiences align with these aspects.

- **Consider the Company's Goals:** Think about the company's short-term and long-term goals. What are they trying to achieve as an organization? How does the role you're interviewing for contribute to these goals? Understanding this alignment can help you formulate relevant questions.

- **Brainstorm Your Questions:** Based on your research, jot down a list of questions that align with the company's mission, the job description, and your own career goals. These questions should seek to uncover information that will help you assess if the company is the right fit for you.

- **Categorize Your Questions**: Group your questions into categories, such as company culture, job expectations, team dynamics, growth opportunities, and challenges. This categorization will help you cover a broad range of topics during the interview.

- **Prioritize Your Questions**: Not all questions are equally important, so prioritize them based on what matters most to you.

Identify the critical questions that must be answered during the interview.

- **Avoid Yes/No Questions**: Craft open-ended questions that encourage discussion and provide you with valuable insights. For example, instead of asking, "Is there room for professional growth?" you could ask, "Can you describe the typical career path for someone in this role?"

- **Prepare Backup Questions**: Sometimes, interviewers may address your questions during the conversation. Have additional questions in your arsenal that you can ask if needed. This demonstrates your preparedness and engagement.

- **Practice Asking Questions**: Practice asking your questions out loud or with a friend or mentor. This will help you become comfortable phrasing your inquiries and ensure they come across as confident and genuine during the interview.

- **Be Attentive During the Interview**: As the interview progresses, pay close attention to the information shared by the interviewer. Tailor your questions based on the context and responses you receive. Ask follow-up questions when appropriate.

• **Respect Time Constraints**: Be mindful of time constraints during the interview. If you have many questions, prioritize them and ask the most crucial ones first. You can always follow up with additional inquiries if time allows.

• **Reflect on Responses**: After the interview, reflect on the responses you received. Did you gain a clear understanding of the company, role, and expectations? Did the answers align with your goals and values?

• **Evaluate Fit**: Consider how the information you gathered aligns with your career aspirations and values. Assess if the company and role are a good fit based on the responses and insights you gained.

Building a targeted questions list is essential for a successful interview. It demonstrates your genuine interest in the role and company while providing you with valuable information to make

informed decisions about your career path.

Chapter 4: The Key to Answering Questions

In this chapter, you will learn the art of answering questions. Equip yourself with techniques like STAR and competency-based responses to ensure you convey your skills and experiences effectively.

Learn the art of answering questions. Equip yourself with techniques like STAR and competency-based responses to ensure you convey your skills and experiences effectively. Learn the art of answering questions. Equip yourself with techniques like STAR and competency-based responses to ensure you convey your skills and experiences effectively. Learn the art of answering questions. Equip yourself with techniques like STAR and competency-based responses to ensure you convey your skills and experiences effectively. Learn the art of answering questions. Equip yourself with techniques like STAR and competency-based responses to ensure you convey your skills and experiences effectively.

4.1 "Tell Me About Yourself": Your Introduction Blueprint

The "Tell Me About Yourself" question is one of the most common and important opening questions in job interviews. It's your opportunity to create a strong first impression and set the tone for the rest of the interview. This section of the book will guide you through crafting a compelling and memorable response to this question.

Your response to "Tell Me About Yourself" should be concise, well-structured, and tailored to the job you're applying for. It's not an invitation to recite your entire life story but rather a chance to highlight your relevant qualifications and experiences. In this chapter, you will learn how to structure your answer effectively, emphasizing key points that align with the job description and the company's needs.

How to effectively introduce:

• **Self-Reflection:** Before your next interview, take some time for self-reflection. Consider your professional journey, including your education, work experiences, achievements, and skills. What sets you apart from other candidates? What do you want the interviewer to remember about you?

• **Customization:** Tailor your response to the specific job you're interviewing for. Identify the skills and qualifications highlighted in the job description and align your introduction with these requirements. Showcase how your background aligns with the company's needs.

• **Structure Your Response**: Use the provided blueprint in this chapter to structure your response effectively. Start with a brief personal introduction, transition into your professional experiences and accomplishments, and conclude by highlighting your enthusiasm for the role and the company.

- **Practice Aloud**: Practice your "Tell Me About Yourself" response aloud, ideally with a friend or mentor who can provide feedback. Focus on clarity, conciseness, and the ability to deliver a confident and engaging introduction.

- **Highlight Achievements**: Emphasize your achievements and their impact. Use specific examples to illustrate your skills and abilities. Quantify your accomplishments whenever possible, as this adds credibility to your response.

- **Relevance and Brevity**: Keep your response relevant to the job and industry. Avoid discussing personal information or unrelated topics. Aim for a response that lasts no longer than two minutes.

- **Feedback and Refinement:** Seek feedback on your introduction from trusted individuals. Consider making adjustments based on their input to enhance the effectiveness of your response.

- **Mindset Shift**: Approach the "Tell Me About Yourself" question as an opportunity to convey your value and fit for the role. Embrace the chance to engage the interviewer and pique their interest in your candidacy.

Remember, a well-crafted response to this question can leave a lasting positive impression and set a confident tone for the remainder of the interview. It's your introduction blueprint to showcasing your qualifications and making a compelling case for why you're the ideal candidate for the job.

4.2 STAR Technique: Navigating Behavioral Questions

Behavioral questions are a common interview technique used by employers to assess a candidate's past behavior as an indicator of future performance. These questions typically begin with phrases like, "Tell me about a time when..." or "Give me an example of..."

and require candidates to share specific experiences from their past. The STAR (Situation, Task, Action, Result) technique is a powerful framework for responding to behavioral questions effectively.

The STAR technique helps you provide structured and comprehensive answers by breaking down your response into four key components:

- **Situation:** Describe the context or situation where the experience occurred.

- **Task:** Explain the specific task or challenge you were facing in that situation.

- **Action:** Detail the actions you took to address the task or challenge.

- **Result:** Summarize the outcomes and results of your actions, focusing on the positive impact.

The advantages of using the STAR technique include:

- **Clarity:** It provides a clear and organized structure for your answers, making them easy for the interviewer to follow.

- **Completeness:** By addressing all four components, you ensure that your response is thorough and covers all necessary details.

- **Relevance:** It helps you stay focused on the specific skills and experiences relevant to the job you're applying for.

- **Impact:** Highlighting positive results demonstrates your ability to make a meaningful impact in previous roles.

How to leverage the STAR technique:

- **Learn the STAR Technique:** Familiarize yourself with the STAR technique by understanding each component—Situation, Task, Action, and Result. Recognize how it can help you structure your responses effectively.

- **Identify Key Experiences:** Review the job description and identify the key competencies and skills the employer is seeking.

Then, recall relevant experiences from your past that demonstrate these qualities.

• **Practice Storytelling:** Practice crafting STAR-based stories for various behavioral questions. Choose experiences that showcase your strengths and align with the job requirements.

• **Tailor Responses:** Customize your STAR responses for each interview based on the specific questions asked and the nuances of the role you're pursuing.

• **Quantify Impact:** When discussing results, quantify your achievements whenever possible. Use numbers, percentages, or specific examples to illustrate the positive outcomes of your actions.

• **Rehearse Aloud:** Practice delivering your STAR responses aloud to ensure clarity, conciseness, and confidence. Consider rehearsing with a friend or mentor who can provide feedback.

• **Seek Feedback:** Ask for feedback on your STAR responses to identify areas for improvement. Adjust your storytelling and emphasize the most compelling aspects of each experience.

- **Build a Repertoire:** Develop a repertoire of STAR stories that cover a range of competencies and experiences. This allows you to respond effectively to a variety of behavioral questions.

By mastering the STAR technique, you'll be well-prepared to navigate behavioral questions with poise and precision during interviews. Your structured and results-oriented responses will demonstrate your qualifications, problem-solving abilities, and the value you bring to potential employers.

4.3 Competency-Based Questions: A Deeper Dive

In this section, we take a deeper dive into competency-based questions, a commonly used interview format that assesses your specific skills, behaviors, and abilities relevant to the job you're applying for. We'll explore what competency-based questions are, why employers rely on them, and how you can prepare to excel when faced with these inquiries.

Competency-based questions provide interviewers with valuable insights into your suitability for a role. Understanding and effectively responding to these questions is essential for several reasons:

- **Alignment with Job Requirements**: Competency-based questions directly relate to the specific skills and competencies required for the job. A thorough grasp of this interview format ensures that your responses are tailored to the role's demands.

- **Behavioral Assessment**: Employers use these questions to evaluate how candidates have demonstrated key competencies in past situations. Your answers showcase your ability to handle similar challenges in the future.

- **Comprehensive Evaluation**: Competency-based questions allow interviewers to assess a wide range of skills, including communication, problem-solving, teamwork, leadership, adaptability, and more. Excelling in these questions can set you apart from other candidates.

How to effectively answer competency-based questions:

• **Identify Targeted Competencies**: Review the job description and identify the competencies and skills crucial for success in the role. Pay close attention to keywords and phrases that indicate the desired qualities.

• **Reflect on Past Experiences:** Recall specific experiences from your professional or personal life where you demonstrated these competencies. These real-life examples will form the basis of your responses.

• **Understand the STAR Technique:** Revisit the STAR (Situation, Task, Action, Result) technique, which is valuable for structuring your responses to competency-based questions. Ensure you can apply this framework effectively.

- **Practice Behavioral Interviewing:** Practice answering competency-based questions using the examples you prepared. Focus on providing context, describing the actions you took, and highlighting the positive outcomes.

- **Quantify Achievements:** Whenever possible, quantify your achievements in your responses. Use metrics, numbers, and specific details to illustrate your impact in previous roles.

- **Feedback and Improvement:** Seek feedback on your responses from mentors, peers, or career advisors. Their insights can help you refine your storytelling and emphasize the most compelling aspects.

- **Diversity of Examples**: Develop a repertoire of competency-based stories that cover a wide range of competencies and scenarios. This ensures you're prepared for a variety of questions.

- **Align with STAR:** Ensure that your responses align with the STAR framework. Practice organizing your answers around the four components: Situation, Task, Action, and Result.

By proactively engaging with the content of this chapter and taking these actions, you'll be well-prepared to navigate competency-based questions in interviews. Your ability to provide specific, evidence-based responses will convey your competence and suitability for the position, increasing your chances of success in the interview process.

4.4 Strengths and Weaknesses: Honesty and Growth

In this section, we delve into the vital topic of assessing your strengths and weaknesses. Understanding and articulating your strengths with honesty and embracing your weaknesses as opportunities for growth are crucial in any interview setting. We'll explore how to analyze your strengths and weaknesses effectively and how this self-awareness can empower you in interviews.

- **Self-Reflection**: Recognizing your strengths allows you to present yourself confidently during interviews, aligning your qualifications with the role's requirements.

- **Growth Mindset:** Acknowledging your weaknesses and areas for improvement demonstrates a growth mindset, a highly valued trait in the professional world.

- **Interview Strategy:** Understanding your strengths enables you to showcase relevant skills and achievements. Acknowledging your weaknesses positions you to address potential concerns proactively.

Strategy for answering strength and weakness questions:

- **Strengths Analysis:**

o   Identify your core strengths by reflecting on your accomplishments, skills, and feedback from peers and supervisors.

o   Consider using self-assessment tools or personality tests to gain deeper insights into your strengths.

o   Prioritize your strengths based on their relevance to the job you're pursuing.

- **Weaknesses Evaluation**:

o   Honestly assess your weaknesses, focusing on areas where you can improve.

o   Seek feedback from mentors, colleagues, or performance evaluations to identify blind spots.

o   Avoid generic responses like "I'm a perfectionist" when discussing weaknesses.

- **Honesty in Interviews:**

o   Be truthful when discussing your strengths and weaknesses in interviews. Authenticity builds trust with interviewers.

o   Use specific examples to illustrate your strengths, showcasing how they've benefited your previous roles.

- **Growth Mindset:**

o   Embrace your weaknesses as opportunities for growth. Highlight your dedication to self-improvement.

o   Share instances where you've actively worked on addressing weaknesses and the positive outcomes.

- **Addressing Weaknesses:**

o   When discussing weaknesses, outline actionable steps you've taken or plan to take to overcome them.

o   Connect weaknesses to skills or competencies relevant to the job and explain your strategy for improvement.

- **Relevance to the Role:**

  o   Tailor your strengths and weaknesses discussion to align with the job's requirements and the organization's culture.

- **Practice Responses:**

  o   Practice articulating your strengths and weaknesses in a clear, concise manner. Avoid lengthy explanations.

  o   Ensure your responses reflect self-awareness and a commitment to continuous growth.

- **Feedback and Self-Improvement:**

  o   Continuously seek feedback from interviews to refine your responses and presentation.

  o   Invest in personal and professional development to enhance your strengths and address weaknesses.

By taking these actions, you'll not only gain a deeper understanding of your strengths and weaknesses but also learn how to present them effectively in interviews. This chapter equips you with the tools to demonstrate honesty, self-awareness, and a growth-oriented mindset, make a positive impression on interviewers, and position yourself as a valuable candidate.

Chapter 5: Technical Interviews Demystified

In this chapter, you will navigate the world of technical interviews. From conquering coding challenges to mastering system design, approach the unique aspects of technical assessments with confidence.

5.1 Tackling the Technical Interview Landscape

In this section, we'll dive into the world of technical interviews—an integral part of many job selection processes, especially in technology-related fields. We'll explore how to approach technical interviews, conduct effective research, and prepare thoroughly to ensure success.

Why It's Important:

- **Technical Proficiency**: Many roles require specific technical skills. A technical interview assesses your ability to apply these skills in real-world scenarios.

- **Competitive Advantage**: Excelling in technical interviews sets you apart from other candidates and showcases your readiness for the role.

- **Confidence Boost**: Adequate preparation instills confidence, allowing you to perform your best under interview pressure.

How to prepare?

- **Understanding Technical Interviews**:

  o Familiarize yourself with the types of technical interviews commonly used in your field, such as coding interviews, system design interviews, or case studies.

o   Research the format, duration, and expectations associated with each type of technical interview.

- **Research the Company and Role**:

o   Gain insights into the company's tech stack, projects, and technical challenges by studying its website, blog posts, and recent news.

o   Understand the specific technical requirements outlined in the job description.

- **Technical Knowledge Review**:

o   Assess your technical knowledge and skills relevant to the role. Identify areas that require improvement.

o   Utilize online resources, textbooks, courses, or coding platforms to refresh and enhance your skills.

- **Practice Coding and Problem-Solving**:

o   For coding interviews, practice solving coding challenges on platforms like LeetCode, HackerRank, or CodeSignal.

o   Focus on algorithms, data structures, and problem-solving techniques.

- **System Design Preparation:**

o   If the role involves system design interviews, study system architecture principles, and design patterns.

o   Practice creating high-level system diagrams and explaining your design choices.

- **Case Study Analysis**:

o   For case study interviews, review relevant industry case studies and practice analyzing complex scenarios.

o   Develop a structured approach to dissecting and solving case study problems.

- **Mock Interviews**:

- Conduct mock technical interviews with peers and mentors or through online platforms.

- Solicit feedback to identify areas for improvement.

- **Communication Skills**:

  - In technical interviews, effective communication is key. Practice explaining your thought process clearly and concisely.

  - Be prepared to defend your decisions and consider alternatives.

- **Time Management**:

  - During technical interviews, time is limited. Practice time management strategies to ensure you can complete tasks within the allotted time.

- **Continuous Learning**:

  - Keep up-to-date with industry trends and emerging technologies relevant to your field.

o   Embrace a mindset of lifelong learning and

adaptability.

By taking these actions, you'll be well-prepared to tackle technical

interviews with confidence and competence. Remember that

technical interviews are an opportunity to showcase your skills and

problem-solving abilities. Thorough preparation and ongoing

learning will significantly enhance your chances of success in this

competitive landscape.

5.2 Coding Challenges and Algorithmic Prowess

This section delves into the world of coding challenges and

algorithmic problem-solving, which are essential components of

technical interviews, particularly in software engineering and

related fields. We will explore how to approach coding challenges,

develop algorithmic prowess, and excel in this critical aspect of

technical interviews.

Why It's Important:

- **Technical Competency:** Coding challenges assess your ability to write clean, efficient code and solve complex problems, reflecting your technical competence.

- **Problem-Solving Skills**: They evaluate your problem-solving and critical-thinking abilities, which are crucial in real-world scenarios.

- **Coding Interviews:** Many technical interviews include coding rounds, making proficiency in this area a significant factor in your success.

How to achieve coding supremacy:

- **Understanding Coding Challenges:**

  o Familiarize yourself with the types of coding challenges you may encounter, such as data structures, algorithms, or coding puzzles.

o   Recognize the formats commonly used, such as online coding platforms or on-site whiteboard coding.

- **Coding Practice:**

o   Dedicate time to regular coding practice on platforms like LeetCode, HackerRank, CodeSignal, or TopCoder.

o   Begin with easy problems and gradually progress to more challenging ones.

- **Data Structures and Algorithms:**

o   Study fundamental data structures (e.g., arrays, linked lists, trees) and algorithms (e.g., sorting, searching) commonly used in coding interviews.

o   Understand when and how to apply specific data structures and algorithms to solve different types of problems.

- **Problem-Solving Strategies:**

o   Develop a systematic problem-solving approach, which may include breaking problems into smaller parts, considering edge cases, and devising efficient solutions.

- **Time Complexity Analysis:**

    o   Learn to analyze the time complexity of your code and optimize it for efficiency.

    o   Understand the Big O notation and how to apply it.

- **Mock Coding Interviews:**

    o   Conduct mock coding interviews with peers or mentors to simulate the interview experience.

    o   Practice explaining your thought process while coding.

- **Feedback and Review:**

    o   Seek feedback on your code quality, problem-solving approach, and efficiency.

o   Review your solutions, especially for problems you found challenging.

- **Language Proficiency:**

o   Master the programming language you'll use during interviews.

o   Be fluent in its syntax and built-in libraries.

- **Consistency is Key:**

o   Consistent practice is more effective than occasional intense study sessions. Dedicate time regularly to coding challenges.

To excel in coding challenges and develop algorithmic prowess, commit to regular practice and systematic improvement. Start with simpler problems and gradually tackle more complex ones. Seek feedback and continuously refine your problem-solving skills. Remember, proficiency in coding and algorithms is not only essential for technical interviews but also for your overall growth as a problem solver and software engineer.

5.3 System Design Interviews: Architecting Solutions

In this chapter, we will dive into the world of System Design Interviews, a critical component of technical interviews. These interviews assess your ability to design scalable and efficient systems, a skill highly sought after in technology companies.

How to Prepare:

- **Understand the Basics:** Start by understanding the fundamental principles of system design. Familiarize yourself with key concepts like scalability, redundancy, load balancing, and database management.

- **Study Real-World Systems:** Analyze real-world systems and their architectures. Learn from the designs of popular platforms like Google, Facebook, or Amazon. Understand how they handle massive user loads and data.

- **Practice Problem Solving:** Solve system design problems regularly. Platforms like LeetCode, HackerRank, and Grokking the System Design Interview offer a plethora of practice questions. Practice designing systems from scratch and refining existing ones.

- **Learn from Others:** Engage with the tech community. Read blogs, watch YouTube videos, or join forums where experienced engineers discuss system design. Learning from others' experiences can be incredibly valuable.

- **Mock Interviews:** Arrange mock system design interviews with peers or mentors. This provides an opportunity to receive feedback and improve your design skills.

- **Document Your Solutions:** When you complete a system design question, document your approach and design choices. This documentation will help you during the actual interview and can serve as a valuable reference.

Call for Action:

- **Start Practicing:** Begin your journey by selecting a system design problem and attempting to design a solution. Remember, practice makes perfect.

- **Explore Resources:** Explore online resources, courses, and books dedicated to system design. Invest time in learning and gaining insights from experts in the field.

- **Join Communities:** Join online communities or forums where you can discuss system design with like-minded individuals. Engaging in discussions can broaden your knowledge.

- **Schedule Mock Interviews**: Don't hesitate to schedule mock interviews to gauge your progress. Constructive feedback from others can be instrumental in your growth.

System Design Interviews may appear daunting at first, but with consistent practice and a solid understanding of the principles, you can excel in these interviews. Your ability to architect solutions will not only impress interviewers but also demonstrate your readiness for complex technical roles. So, roll up your sleeves and embark on your journey to master system design.

5.4 Case Studies and Real-World Problem Solving

In this chapter, we venture into the realm of case studies and real-world problem-solving in technical interviews. These interviews require you to apply your technical knowledge to practical scenarios, mirroring the challenges you might face in a professional setting.

How to Excel in Case Studies:

• **Master the Basics:** Before delving into case studies, ensure you have a strong foundation in the relevant technical concepts. Understand the principles, algorithms, and data structures that are commonly used in your field.

• **Practice Scenario-Based Problems:** Seek out case study-style problems from books, online platforms, or interview preparation courses. These problems often present complex scenarios and require you to devise solutions.

• **Develop a Problem-Solving Framework:** Create a systematic approach for tackling case studies. This might involve breaking down the problem, identifying constraints, and outlining possible solutions.

• **Think Aloud:** During interviews, articulate your thought process. Explain your approach, assumptions, and reasoning as you work through the case study. Interviewers value clarity in your problem-solving journey.

- **Consider Trade-offs:** Real-world problems often involve trade-offs between different solutions. Understand when to prioritize factors like efficiency, scalability, or simplicity.

- **Ask Questions:** Don't hesitate to seek clarification from the interviewer. Effective communication is crucial in understanding the problem thoroughly.

The Importance of Real-World Problem Solving:

Real-world problems mirror the challenges you'll encounter in your professional career. Mastering case studies and practical scenarios showcases your ability to apply theoretical knowledge to solve complex, practical issues. It demonstrates your readiness for the demands of the job.

Call for Action:

- **Problem-Solving Practice:** Start practicing case studies and real-world scenarios regularly. The more exposure you have, the more comfortable you'll become.

- **Problem Decomposition:** Develop the skill of breaking down complex problems into manageable components. This approach simplifies the problem-solving process.

- **Effective Communication:** Practice explaining your thought process clearly and concisely. Consider recording your practice sessions to review your communication skills.

- **Learn from Experience:** If you encounter challenging scenarios at work or during internships, reflect on them. Consider how you could have approached the problems differently. Real-world experience is a valuable teacher.

- **Stay Updated:** Technology evolves, and new challenges emerge. Stay updated with the latest trends and technologies in your field to be well-prepared for case study interviews.

Case studies and real-world problem-solving are opportunities to showcase your practical skills and problem-solving prowess. Embrace these challenges with enthusiasm, and you'll not only excel in interviews but also thrive in your future technical roles.

Chapter 6: Confidence and Nerve Management

In this chapter, Delve into the psychology of interview anxiety and explore confidence-building strategies. Learn to maintain composure even in high-pressure situations.

6.1 The Psychology of Interview Anxiety:

Interview anxiety is a natural response to the pressure of the situation. It can manifest in various ways, such as nervousness, sweaty palms, racing thoughts, or even mental blocks. Understanding the psychology behind interview anxiety is the first step in managing it.

How to Handle Interview Anxiety:

- **Preparation is Key**: One of the most effective ways to combat anxiety is thorough preparation. The more you know about the company, the role, and the interview format, the more confident you'll feel. Research, practice, and rehearse extensively.

- **Breathing Techniques:** Deep, controlled breathing can help calm your nerves. Practice diaphragmatic breathing to slow your heart rate and reduce anxiety.

- **Visualization:** Imagine yourself in a successful interview scenario. Visualization techniques can boost your confidence and create a positive mindset.

- **Positive Self-Talk:** Replace negative thoughts with positive affirmations. Remind yourself of your skills, experiences, and past successes. Affirmations can be powerful confidence boosters.

- **Mock Interviews:** Conduct mock interviews with friends, family, or mentors. This provides a safe space to practice and receive constructive feedback.

- **Mindfulness and Relaxation:** Techniques like meditation and mindfulness can help you stay centered and reduce anxiety. Dedicate time to relaxation exercises before the interview.

- **Focus on the Present**: Instead of dwelling on what might happen, concentrate on the present moment. Listen actively to the interviewer's questions and respond thoughtfully.

- **Accept Imperfection:** Understand that nobody is perfect. It's okay to make minor mistakes during interviews. What matters is how you recover and continue.

- **Seek Professional Help:** If interview anxiety is severely affecting your performance, consider consulting a therapist or counselor who specializes in anxiety management.

Call for Action:

- **Preparation Rituals:** Develop a pre-interview routine that includes last-minute review, relaxation exercises, and positive affirmations.

- **Breathing Exercises:** Practice deep breathing techniques daily to make them second nature. Use them not only in interviews but also in other anxiety-inducing situations.

- **Mock Interviews:** Engage in regular mock interviews to simulate the interview experience. Solicit honest feedback to identify areas for improvement.

- **Visualization:** Dedicate time to visualize successful interviews. Imagine yourself confidently answering questions and impressing the interviewers.

- **Mindfulness Practice:** Incorporate mindfulness and relaxation exercises into your daily routine to manage anxiety in all aspects of life.

By addressing the psychology of interview anxiety and adopting effective coping strategies, you can enhance your confidence and composure during interviews. Remember that interview anxiety is a common challenge, and with practice and self-care, you can overcome it and perform at your best.

6.2 Confidence-Building Strategies

Confidence is the secret ingredient that can transform an average interviewee into an impressive one. In this chapter, we'll explore a range of strategies to boost your self-assurance and shine during job interviews.

Understanding the Role of Confidence:

Confidence is your silent advocate in the interview room. It's the assurance you convey in your abilities, experiences, and potential. When you exude confidence, you inspire trust in the minds of interviewers, making them more likely to see you as an ideal candidate.

Confidence-Building Strategies:

- **Know Your Value**: Start by recognizing your worth. Reflect on your skills, achievements, and the unique qualities that

93

set you apart. Acknowledge your strengths and embrace your potential.

- **Positive Self-Talk**: Challenge negative thoughts with positive affirmations. Replace self-doubt with statements like, "I am well-prepared," "I have the skills needed for this role," and "I am a strong candidate."

- **Preparation is Empowerment:** The more prepared you are, the more confident you'll feel. Research the company, thoroughly understand the job description, and practice your responses to common interview questions.

- **Body Language Mastery**: Your body language can convey confidence. Maintain good posture, make eye contact, and offer a firm handshake. These non-verbal cues can speak volumes about your self-assuredness.

- **Visualization**: Picture yourself excelling in the interview. Visualize the interview room, the interviewers, and your confident responses. This mental rehearsal can boost your actual performance.

- **Practice, Practice, Practice**: Engage in mock interviews with peers, mentors, or career coaches. The more you practice, the more comfortable and confident you'll become in interview scenarios.

- **Learning from Failure**: Understand that setbacks are part of the journey. Instead of dwelling on past interview failures, view them as opportunities for growth. Analyze what went wrong and use those insights to improve.

- **Breathing Techniques**: Deep, slow breaths can calm nerves and bolster confidence. Practice deep breathing exercises before and during interviews to maintain composure.

- **Celebrate Achievements**: Keep a record of your accomplishments and milestones. Celebrate your successes, no matter how small. These reminders can bolster your self-esteem.

Call for Action:

- **Confidence Journal:** Start a confidence journal to record your achievements, positive affirmations, and instances where you demonstrated self-assuredness.

- **Body Language Practice:** Practice confident body language in front of a mirror. Ask for feedback from friends or family to fine-tune your non-verbal cues.

- **Visualization Ritual:** Dedicate time daily to visualize successful interview scenarios. Imagine yourself confidently responding to questions and impressing interviewers.

- **Positive Affirmations:** Develop a list of empowering affirmations tailored to your interview goals. Recite these affirmations daily to boost self-confidence.

- **Practice Interviews:** Continue to engage in mock interviews, focusing on areas where you want to improve your confidence. Seek constructive feedback to refine your skills.

Confidence is not a fixed trait; it's a skill that can be nurtured and developed. By incorporating these confidence-building strategies into your interview preparation, you'll be better equipped to present your best self during job interviews and make a lasting impression on potential employers. Remember, confidence is a journey, not a destination, and it's within your reach.

6.3 Maintaining Composure Under Pressure

Maintaining composure under pressure is a crucial skill during job interviews. It's natural to feel nervous or anxious, but how you handle these emotions can make all the difference. In this section, we'll explore strategies to help you stay cool, confident, and collected when the heat is on.

Understanding Pressure:

Pressure is a common aspect of job interviews. It arises from the desire to perform well, the fear of making mistakes, or the significance of the opportunity. Recognizing that pressure is a normal part of the process is the first step in managing it effectively.

Strategies for Maintaining Composure:

- **Preparation is Your Best Friend:** Thoroughly prepare for the interview. The more you know about the company, role, and industry, the more confident you'll feel. Practice answering common interview questions to reduce uncertainty.

- **Practice Deep Breathing**: Deep, slow breathing can help calm your nerves. Before the interview, take a few minutes to practice deep breathing exercises. During the interview, if you start feeling overwhelmed, pause and take a deep breath.

- **Positive Self-Talk**: Replace negative thoughts with positive affirmations. Remind yourself of your qualifications, past achievements, and the value you bring to the table. Self-assurance can counteract anxiety.

- **Focus on the Present**: Concentrate on the current moment rather than worrying about the outcome. Pay close attention to the interviewer's questions and your responses. Staying present helps you stay grounded.

- **Visualization Techniques**: Use visualization to mentally rehearse the interview. Imagine yourself confidently answering questions, building rapport with the interviewer, and leaving a positive impression.

- **Effective Time Management**: Plan your schedule with extra time for unexpected delays. Rushing to the interview can exacerbate stress. Arriving early allows you to relax and collect your thoughts.

- **Embrace Imperfections**: Understand that nobody is flawless, and interviews may not always go as planned. Embrace imperfections as opportunities for growth and learning. Interviewers appreciate authenticity.

- **Practice Resilience**: Develop resilience by bouncing back from setbacks. If you encounter a challenging question or feel flustered during an answer, pause, gather your thoughts, and continue confidently.

Taking Action:

- **Deep Breathing Exercises**: Incorporate deep breathing exercises into your daily routine, not just before interviews. It's a valuable skill for managing stress in various situations.

- **Affirmation List**: Create a list of positive affirmations tailored to your strengths and qualities. Review these affirmations before interviews to boost your confidence.

- **Daily Visualization**: Dedicate a few minutes each day to visualize successful interview scenarios. This mental rehearsal can build your resilience and confidence over time.

- **Mindfulness Practice**: Learn mindfulness techniques to stay present and focused during high-pressure moments. Apply these techniques beyond interviews to manage stress in everyday life.

- **Reflect and Learn**: After interviews, reflect on moments when you felt pressure and how you handled it. Use these reflections to refine your pressure-management strategies for future interviews.

Remember, pressure is a sign that you care about the opportunity. With practice and these strategies, you can learn to manage pressure effectively and maintain composure under even the most challenging interview circumstances. This skill will not only help you excel in interviews but also serve you well in your professional journey.

Chapter 7: Etiquette and Professionalism

In this chapter, you will master the art of professionalism. Explore the impact of dressing for success, valuing punctuality, using non-verbal communication effectively, and crafting the perfect interview follow-up.

7.1 Dressing for Success

In the world of job interviews, appearances do matter. Your attire is one of the first aspects of your personal brand that interviewers notice, and it plays a significant role in shaping their initial impression of you. This section explores the importance of dressing for success, provides guidance on appropriate interview attire, and offers tips to ensure you make a polished and professional appearance.

The Significance of Dressing for Success:

Your clothing choices communicate more than you might think during an interview. Here's why dressing appropriately is vital:

- **First Impressions:** Your attire is one of the first things interviewers notice about you. A well-groomed appearance can create a positive initial impression.

- **Professionalism:** Dressing professionally demonstrates your respect for the opportunity and the interviewer. It conveys that you take the interview seriously.

- **Cultural Fit:** Different companies have various dress codes and corporate cultures. Dressing appropriately helps you align with the company's expectations.

- **Confidence Boost:** When you look good, you often feel more confident. Confidence can positively impact your interview performance.

Guidelines for Interview Attire:

- **Research the Company Culture:** Before the interview, research the company's culture and dress code. If in doubt, it's generally better to be slightly overdressed than underdressed.

- **Classic vs. Creative**: Opt for classic, timeless attire. For most interviews, conservative clothing choices are safer than bold, creative ones.

- **Professional Wardrobe Essentials:**

  o   Suits: For formal interviews, wear a well-fitted suit in a neutral color like black, navy, or charcoal gray.

  o   Shirts: Choose a clean, well-pressed dress shirt in a subtle color.

  o   Ties: If you wear a tie, opt for a conservative pattern or color.

  o   Footwear: Wear closed-toe, polished shoes that match your outfit.

o   Accessories: Keep accessories minimal and understated.

- **Grooming Matters:** Pay attention to personal grooming. Ensure your hair, nails, and overall appearance are tidy and well-maintained.

- **Fit is Key**: Ensure your clothing fits well. Clothes that are too tight or too loose can be distracting and uncomfortable.

- **Avoid Distractions:** Minimize distracting elements, such as loud patterns or flashy accessories. Your attire should not overshadow your qualifications.

Taking Action:

- **Wardrobe Selection:** Choose interview outfits in advance and ensure they are clean and well-maintained.

- **Dress Rehearsal:** Try on your interview attire to confirm it fits well and looks polished.

- **Company Research:** Investigate the company's dress code and culture to tailor your attire accordingly.

- **Grooming Checklist:** Develop a grooming routine that covers hair, skincare, and overall presentation.

- **Feedback:** Seek feedback on your interview outfit from friends, family, or mentors to ensure it conveys professionalism.

- **Prepare Wardrobe Options:** Have backup clothing options ready in case of unexpected wardrobe malfunctions.

Remember that dressing for success is not just about adhering to a dress code; it's about making a positive, professional impression. Your attire should complement your qualifications and skills, not detract from them. By following these guidelines and taking action, you can confidently present yourself as a polished and professional candidate during interviews.

7.2 Punctuality and Time Management

Punctuality is a fundamental aspect of professionalism that should not be underestimated. Being on time for interviews and other professional engagements reflects your commitment, reliability, and respect for others' time. In this section, we explore the importance of punctuality, share strategies for effective time management, and emphasize its impact on interview success.

The Significance of Punctuality:

- **First Impressions:** Arriving on time creates a positive first impression. It demonstrates your commitment to the interview process and your respect for the interviewer's schedule.

- **Professionalism:** Punctuality is a hallmark of professionalism. Employers value candidates who can manage their time effectively, as it often translates to better job performance.

- **Stress Reduction:** Being punctual reduces stress. Arriving late can lead to anxiety, which may negatively affect your interview performance.

- **Demonstrating Reliability:** Punctuality showcases your reliability. Employers seek individuals they can depend on to meet deadlines and fulfill responsibilities.

Strategies for Effective Time Management:

- **Plan Ahead:** Prepare for your interview well in advance. Research the interview location, consider traffic or commute times, and plan your route. Aim to arrive 10-15 minutes early.

- **Use Technology:** Utilize navigation apps or GPS to estimate travel times accurately. Set alarms or reminders to ensure you leave with sufficient buffer time.

- **Account for Contingencies:** Unexpected delays can occur. Plan for potential traffic jams, public transportation delays, or other unforeseen circumstances by leaving early.

- **Dress Quickly:** Lay out your interview attire the night before to minimize morning stress. Dress quickly and double-check your appearance before leaving.

- **Practice Punctuality:** Punctuality is a habit. Practice being on time for all your commitments, not just interviews, to reinforce this skill.

- **Time Blocking:** Use time-blocking techniques to allocate specific time slots for interview preparation, travel, and the actual interview. Stick to your schedule diligently.

Taking Action:

- **Schedule Alerts:** Set reminders or alarms on your phone to notify you when it's time to leave for the interview location.

- **Test the Route:** If possible, perform a trial run to the interview location before the actual day. Familiarity with the route can reduce anxiety.

- **Early Arrival:** Aim to arrive at the interview location at least 10-15 minutes early. Use this extra time to relax, review your notes, and mentally prepare.

- **Professionalism in Waiting:** If you arrive significantly early, wait patiently in a nearby café or waiting area. Avoid arriving too early at the company's reception.

- **Courtesy Calls:** If you anticipate being delayed due to unforeseen circumstances, call the interviewer promptly to inform them and provide an updated estimated arrival time.

- **Reflect on Time Management:** Regularly assess your time management skills and identify areas for improvement. Seek feedback from mentors or peers on your punctuality.

Punctuality is an asset in your professional journey. It not only enhances your chances of interview success but also sets a strong foundation for a reliable and dependable professional reputation. By prioritizing punctuality and implementing effective time management strategies, you demonstrate your commitment to excellence and create a positive impression throughout your career.

7.3 Non-Verbal Communication and Body Language

Effective communication goes beyond words. Non-verbal cues and body language play a crucial role in conveying your professionalism, confidence, and engagement during interviews and in your career. In this section, we explore the significance of non-verbal communication and provide guidance on harnessing the power of body language to your advantage.

Understanding Non-Verbal Communication:

- **Facial Expressions:** Your face is a powerful communicator. Maintain a pleasant and approachable facial expression to convey warmth and interest. Avoid frowning or appearing disinterested.

- **Eye Contact:** Establish and maintain eye contact with your interviewer. It demonstrates confidence and shows that you are attentive and engaged in the conversation.

- **Gestures:** Use natural and purposeful hand gestures to emphasize points. Avoid excessive or distracting movements, as they can detract from your message.

- **Posture:** Maintain an upright and confident posture. Slouching or hunching can convey a lack of interest or confidence.

- **Handshakes:** Offer a firm and confident handshake when greeting your interviewer. A weak or overly strong handshake can send the wrong impression.

- **Personal Space:** Respect personal space boundaries. Avoid standing or sitting too close, as it can make others uncomfortable.

The Impact of Body Language:

- **Confidence:** Strong and positive body language exudes confidence. It can instill confidence in your interviewer and convey that you are well-prepared.

- **Engagement:** Active listening through body language, such as nodding in agreement or leaning forward slightly, demonstrates your interest in the conversation.

- **Trustworthiness:** Consistent and sincere non-verbal cues contribute to building trust. They signal that you are genuine and trustworthy.

- **Professionalism:** Professional body language reinforces your commitment to the interview and the potential role.

Effective Use of Non-Verbal Communication:

- **Practice Self-Awareness:** Pay attention to your own body language during practice interviews or mock sessions. Identify areas for improvement and work on them.

- **Mirror Your Interviewer:** Subtly mirroring your interviewer's body language can create a sense of rapport. However, be genuine and avoid overdoing it.

- **Control Nervous Habits:** Nervous habits like tapping your foot or playing with your hair can be distracting. Identify and control these habits during interviews.

- **Prepare and Rehearse:** Prepare answers to common interview questions and rehearse them with attention to your body language. Practice with a friend or mentor for feedback.

Taking Action:

- **Video Self-Assessment:** Record yourself answering interview questions on video. Review the footage to identify areas where your body language can be improved.

- **Mock Interviews:** Conduct mock interviews with a mentor or career coach who can provide real-time feedback on your non-verbal communication.

- **Regular Self-Evaluation:** Continuously assess and refine your non-verbal communication skills. Self-awareness is key to improvement.

- **Observe Others:** Pay attention to the body language of successful professionals and leaders. Learn from their cues and gestures.

Effective non-verbal communication and body language can enhance your interview performance and leave a lasting positive impression. By mastering these skills, you can convey confidence, engagement, and professionalism, ultimately positioning yourself as a top candidate in the eyes of potential employers.

7.4 The Perfect Interview Follow-Up

The interview doesn't end when you walk out of the room. In fact, the period after the interview is a critical phase that can significantly impact your chances of success. The Perfect

Interview Follow-Up entails a series of strategic actions that demonstrate your continued interest, professionalism, and gratitude.

The Importance of a Follow-Up:

- **Reinforce Your Interest:** Sending a follow-up message or note reaffirms your enthusiasm for the role and the company.

- **Demonstrate Professionalism:** A well-crafted follow-up reflects your professionalism and attention to detail.

- **Clarify Any Misunderstandings:** It's an opportunity to address any concerns or clarify points discussed during the interview.

- **Stay Top of Mind:** Your follow-up keeps you in the interviewer's thoughts as they make their decision.

Taking Action:

- **Thank-You Note:** Send a personalized thank-you email within 24 hours of the interview. Express gratitude for the opportunity, reaffirm your interest in the role, and mention a specific detail from the interview to show your attentiveness.

- **Reiterate Value:** Emphasize how your skills and qualifications align with the job requirements and how you can contribute to the company's success.

- **Address Concerns:** If there were any concerns or points of clarification discussed during the interview, address them in a positive and solution-oriented manner.

- **Stay Concise:** Keep your follow-up message concise and to the point. Avoid overwhelming the interviewer with lengthy emails.

- **Personalization:** Whenever possible, personalize your follow-up by mentioning specific discussions or moments from the interview. This shows that you were fully engaged.

- **Multiple Points of Contact:** If there were multiple interviewers, send individual thank-you notes to each one. Be sure to customize the content for each recipient.

Sample Follow-Up Email:

Subject: Thank You for the Interview

Dear [Interviewer's Name],

I wanted to express my sincere gratitude for the opportunity to interview for the [Job Title] position at [Company Name]. It was a pleasure to learn more about your team and the exciting projects you have in store.

Our discussion about [specific topic discussed during the interview] further ignited my enthusiasm for the role, and I'm even more eager to contribute my skills and experience to your organization. I believe that my background in [mention relevant skills/experience] aligns perfectly with the needs of the team.

If there are any additional details or questions you'd like to discuss, please don't hesitate to reach out. I'm here to provide any further information you may require.

Once again, thank you for your time and consideration. I look forward to the possibility of joining [Company Name] and contributing to your continued success.

Best regards,

In-Person Follow-Up:

If the interview process involves an in-person follow-up, such as sending a handwritten thank-you card, ensure that it is legible and professional and expresses gratitude and enthusiasm.

By mastering the art of the perfect interview follow-up, you leave a positive and lasting impression that can set you apart from other candidates. It demonstrates your professionalism, attention to detail, and commitment to the opportunity, ultimately strengthening your candidacy for the position.

Chapter 8: Negotiating Your Worth

In this Chapter, you will unlock the secrets of salary negotiation. Evaluate job offers holistically and gain insights into compensation packages and successful negotiation techniques.

8.1 The Art of Salary Negotiation:

Salary negotiation is a crucial aspect of the job interview process that often determines your compensation and benefits package. This section explores the art of salary negotiation, providing you with insights, strategies, and actions to secure a compensation package that aligns with your skills, experience, and market value.

Understanding the Importance of Salary Negotiation:

- **Maximizing Your Value:** Effective negotiation allows you to receive the best possible compensation, ensuring that your skills and contributions are appropriately rewarded.

- **Securing Your Financial Future:** A higher salary can have a significant impact on your financial stability and long-term goals, such as savings, investments, and retirement planning.

- **Career Growth:** Negotiating a competitive salary sets a positive precedent for your future earnings, as subsequent raises and bonuses are often calculated based on your initial salary.

- **Job Satisfaction:** Fair compensation contributes to job satisfaction, motivation, and a sense of value within the organization.

Call for action:

- **Preparation:** Research industry salary benchmarks, understand the company's compensation structure and evaluate your own skills and experience. Determine your minimum acceptable salary, target salary, and ideal salary.

- **Timing:** Initiate salary discussions after you've received a job offer. Avoid discussing compensation too early in the interview process; instead, focus on showcasing your qualifications.

- **Express Enthusiasm:** When discussing salary, express your enthusiasm for the role and the company before diving into compensation details. This demonstrates your commitment to the opportunity.

- **Base Salary vs. Benefits:** Consider the entire compensation package, including base salary, bonuses, stock options, benefits, and other perks. Don't fixate solely on the base salary.

- **Negotiation Techniques:** Use effective negotiation techniques, such as anchoring (starting with a higher number), mirroring (reflecting the employer's language), and making a compelling case based on your skills and market value.

- **Be Prepared to Counteroffer:** If the initial offer is below your expectations, be prepared to counteroffer with a well-reasoned argument and supporting data.

- **Consider Non-Financial Benefits:** Negotiation isn't just about money. Consider negotiating for additional paid time off, flexible work hours, professional development opportunities, or other non-financial benefits that matter to you.

- **Maintain Professionalism:** Regardless of the negotiation outcome, maintain professionalism and gratitude. Remember that negotiation is a two-way process, and both parties should feel satisfied with the result.

Sample Salary Negotiation Script:

"Thank you for extending the job offer for the [Job Title] position. I'm excited about the opportunity to join [Company Name] and contribute to [specific project or team]. I've thoroughly reviewed

the offer, and I believe that my skills and experience align well with the role's responsibilities.

While I'm enthusiastic about the position, I was hoping to discuss the possibility of adjusting the compensation package. Based on my research and market standards for this role, I was anticipating a salary range of [your desired range]. Is there flexibility in the salary offered, or can we explore other aspects of the compensation package?

I want to emphasize my commitment to the role and the company's success. I believe that aligning the compensation with industry standards will ensure a mutually beneficial partnership. I'm open to discussing this further and finding a solution that works for both parties.

Thank you for your understanding and consideration."

By mastering the art of salary negotiation, you can secure a compensation package that reflects your true worth and sets the stage for a successful and rewarding career journey.

8.1 Evaluating Job Offers: Beyond the Paycheck

Evaluating a job offer goes beyond the base salary—it involves assessing the complete compensation package, company culture, career growth opportunities, and alignment with your personal and professional goals. In this section, we delve into the crucial steps of evaluating job offers to make an informed decision.

Understanding the Comprehensive Offer:

- **Salary and Bonuses:** Begin by examining the offered salary, bonuses, and any performance-related incentives. Consider how these financial components align with your financial objectives and lifestyle.

- **Benefits and Perks:** Assess the employee benefits package, including health insurance, retirement plans, stock options, and other perks such as gym memberships, wellness programs, or childcare assistance. These benefits can significantly impact your overall compensation.

- **Work-Life Balance:** Evaluate the company's approach to work-life balance, including flexible work hours, remote work options, and policies on vacation days and personal time off. Determine if these align with your personal priorities.

- **Career Advancement:** Explore the potential for career growth within the organization. Assess whether the role offers opportunities for skill development, promotions, and the chance to take on increased responsibilities.

- **Company Culture:** Research and consider the company's culture, values, and workplace environment. Assess whether the culture aligns with your values and if you can see yourself thriving within that setting.

- **Location and Commute:** Examine the location of the company and the potential commute. Consider how these factors impact your daily life, including travel time and convenience.

Actions to Take When Evaluating Job Offers:

- **Create a Pros and Cons List:** Make a list of the pros and cons of each job offer, including all aspects of compensation, benefits, company culture, and career prospects.

- **Prioritize Your Needs:** Identify your top priorities and must-haves in a job offer. Determine which factors are non-negotiable and which ones you are willing to compromise on.

- **Seek Clarity:** If there are uncertainties or ambiguities in the offer, don't hesitate to seek clarification from the employer. This ensures that you have a complete understanding of the terms.

- **Consult with Trusted Advisors:** Discuss the job offer with mentors, friends, or family members who can provide valuable insights and offer an external perspective.

- **Reflect on Long-Term Goals:** Consider how each job offer aligns with your long-term career goals and aspirations. Assess whether the role provides opportunities for professional growth and development.

- **Negotiate Thoughtfully:** If you decide to negotiate aspects of the offer, approach the negotiation process with professionalism and a focus on mutual benefit.

- **Trust Your Instincts:** Ultimately, trust your instincts and make a decision that feels right for you. Your intuition often plays a vital role in choosing the right career path.

Evaluating job offers requires a comprehensive assessment of all factors, ensuring that your decision aligns with your values, goals, and well-being. By taking a thoughtful and strategic approach, you can make a choice that propels your career in the direction you desire.

8.2 Compensation Packages Unveiled

Understanding the components of a compensation package is essential when evaluating job offers. A compensation package encompasses more than just the base salary; it includes various elements that contribute to your overall financial well-being. In this section, we'll unveil the components of compensation packages and how to assess their value.

Key Elements of Compensation Packages:

- **Base Salary:** The core component of your compensation package is your base salary. It's the fixed amount you'll receive regularly, usually on a monthly or bi-weekly basis. This forms the foundation of your income.

- **Bonuses and Incentives:** Many companies offer bonuses and incentives tied to performance metrics or company goals. These can significantly boost your earnings and provide motivation to excel in your role.

- **Stock Options and Equity:** Some companies offer stock options or equity as part of the compensation package. This can be a valuable long-term investment, potentially allowing you to benefit from the company's growth.

- **Benefits:** Employee benefits can include health insurance, dental and vision coverage, retirement plans (such as 401(k)), life insurance, and disability insurance. Assess the quality and extent of these benefits.

- **Paid Time Off:** Evaluate the company's policy on paid time off (PTO), including vacation days, holidays, and sick leave. Adequate PTO is essential for maintaining a work-life balance.

- **Additional Perks:** Consider any additional perks offered by the company, such as wellness programs, childcare assistance, gym memberships, or commuting benefits.

Assessing the Value of Compensation Packages:

- **Calculate the Total Compensation:** To understand the true value of a compensation package, calculate the total annual compensation by considering the base salary, bonuses, incentives, and the potential value of stock options or equity.

- **Compare with Industry Standards:** Research industry standards and salary benchmarks for your role and level of experience. This provides context for evaluating whether the offer is competitive.

- **Evaluate Benefits:** Pay close attention to the quality and coverage of benefits. A comprehensive benefits package can significantly impact your financial security and well-being.

- **Consider Long-Term Growth:** Assess the potential for long-term financial growth. Stock options and equity can be valuable if the company is poised for growth.

- **Review Vesting Periods:** If stock options or equity are part of the package, review the vesting periods and conditions for exercising these options. Understand the potential financial benefits and risks.

Actions to Take When Evaluating Compensation Packages:

- **Request a Detailed Breakdown:** Ask the employer for a detailed breakdown of the compensation package, including all components and their respective values.

- **Consult with Financial Advisors:** Consider consulting with financial advisors or professionals who can provide insights into the financial implications of the package.

- **Negotiate Thoughtfully:** If you have concerns or if the package doesn't meet your expectations, engage in a thoughtful negotiation process. Focus on mutual benefit and be prepared to make a compelling case.

- **Consider Your Financial Goals:** Reflect on your financial goals, including savings, investments, and debt management, to ensure that the compensation package aligns with your objectives.

- **Evaluate Overall Job Fit:** While compensation is important, don't overlook other factors like job responsibilities, company culture, and career growth opportunities when making your decision.

Understanding and evaluating compensation packages is a critical aspect of the job offer assessment process. It empowers you to make an informed decision that aligns with your financial and career goals, ultimately contributing to your long-term success and well-being.

8.3 Navigating the Negotiation Table

Negotiating your compensation is a pivotal step in securing a job offer that reflects your true worth. In this section, we'll explore the art of negotiation and provide guidance on how to navigate the negotiation table effectively.

Understanding the Negotiation Process:

Negotiating your compensation package is not about demanding more; it's about finding common ground where both you and the employer feel satisfied with the agreement. Here are key aspects to understand about the negotiation process:

• **Timing:** Negotiation typically occurs after you've received a job offer but before you've accepted it. It's a crucial phase, and your approach can influence the final terms.

• **Research:** Conduct thorough research to understand industry salary standards, company practices, and the cost of living in the location where you'll work. Knowledge is your ally in negotiation.

• **Prioritize Interests:** Identify your top priorities and interests in the negotiation. Is it a higher salary, additional benefits, flexible work arrangements, or professional development opportunities?

- **Effective Communication:** Maintain open and respectful communication with the employer throughout the negotiation. Clearly express your needs and concerns while listening to theirs.

- **Negotiation Points:** Your negotiation may involve various components, such as base salary, bonuses, benefits, or stock options. Be prepared to discuss each point.

Actions to Take When Navigating the Negotiation Table:

- **Express Enthusiasm:** Start the conversation by expressing your enthusiasm for the job and your desire to join the organization. This sets a positive tone.

- **Request Time:** If you need time to evaluate the offer, politely request it. Employers often understand the need for thoughtful consideration.

- **Know Your Value:** Use your research to justify your requests. Provide evidence of your skills, experience, and industry benchmarks to support your position.

- **Practice Empathy:** Understand the employer's perspective and constraints. Consider how your requests align with the company's values and financial capabilities.

- **Be Flexible:** Be prepared to compromise. While it's essential to advocate for your interests, flexibility can help reach a mutually beneficial agreement.

- **Consider Non-Salary Components:** Explore other components of the compensation package, such as benefits, work-life balance, or professional development opportunities, which can be negotiated.

- **Get It in Writing:** Once both parties agree on the terms, request a written offer letter or employment contract outlining the agreed-upon compensation package.

- **Seek Legal Advice:** If the negotiation involves complex legal aspects, such as stock options or equity, consider consulting with legal professionals to ensure you fully understand the terms.

- **Maintain Professionalism:** Regardless of the negotiation's outcome, maintain professionalism and gratitude throughout the process. Your reputation matters.

- **Evaluate the Final Offer:** After reaching an agreement, take time to review the final offer in detail before accepting it. Ensure it aligns with your expectations.

Negotiation is a valuable skill that can benefit your career throughout its duration. When done effectively and respectfully, it can lead to a compensation package that reflects your true worth and sets a positive tone for your employment relationship.

Chapter 9: Navigating Special Situations

In this chapter, you will navigate unique interview scenarios. Embrace career changes, resume your journey after a break, conquer virtual interviews, and win over panel interviews.

9.1 Career Changers: Embracing the Unknown

Changing careers can be a bold and transformative decision. This section is dedicated to those who are embarking on a journey to switch careers, providing insights and guidance on how to navigate this significant transition with confidence and purpose.

Understanding the Career Change Process:

Changing your career path involves more than simply switching jobs; it's about redefining your professional identity. Here are key aspects to consider when navigating a career change:

- **Self-Assessment:** Begin by assessing your skills, interests, values, and passions. What do you excel at, and what truly motivates you?

- **Research:** Investigate your desired industry or field thoroughly. Understand its requirements, trends, and potential challenges.

- **Transferable Skills:** Identify skills and experiences from your previous career that can be transferred to your new path. These can be valuable assets.

- **Education and Training:** Depending on your new career choice, you may need to acquire new qualifications or certifications. Plan for any necessary education or training.

- **Networking:** Build connections with professionals in your target industry. Attend networking events, join online forums, and seek informational interviews to gain insights.

- **Resume and Cover Letter:** Tailor your application materials to highlight relevant transferable skills and experiences. Emphasize your motivation for the change.

Actions to Take When Embracing a Career Change:

- **Set Clear Goals:** Define your career change goals, both short-term and long-term. Having a clear vision will help you stay focused and motivated.

- **Seek Guidance:** Consider working with a career coach or mentor who specializes in career transitions. Their expertise can be invaluable.

- **Network Actively:** Attend industry events, join relevant social media groups, and connect with professionals who have successfully made similar career changes.

- **Gain Practical Experience:** Volunteer, intern, or freelance in your desired field to gain hands-on experience and build your new network.

- **Continuous Learning:** Invest in your education and skill development. Take courses, earn certifications, or pursue additional qualifications.

- **Craft Your Story:** Be prepared to explain your career change to potential employers or interviewers. Emphasize how your unique background brings value to your new path.

- **Stay Resilient:** Understand that a career change may come with challenges and setbacks. Maintain resilience and adaptability as you navigate the transition.

- **Embrace Flexibility:** Be open to exploring different roles or entry-level positions in your new field. Flexibility can lead to valuable opportunities.

- **Leverage Transferable Skills:** Showcase transferable skills from your previous career that are relevant to your new path. These skills can set you apart.

- **Stay Informed:** Stay updated on industry trends and developments to demonstrate your commitment and passion for your new career.

Embracing a career change requires courage, determination, and a willingness to embrace the unknown. It's a journey that can lead to personal and professional growth, opening doors to new and exciting opportunities. By taking strategic actions and maintaining a positive outlook, you can successfully transition into a fulfilling new career path.

9.2 Returning to the Workforce: Resuming the Journey

Returning to the workforce after a career break can be a fulfilling and empowering experience. Whether you took time off for family reasons, personal pursuits, or any other purpose, this section provides guidance on how to make a successful reentry into the professional world.

Understanding the Return-to-Work Process:

Returning to work after a hiatus involves a unique set of challenges and opportunities. Here's what to consider when resuming your career journey:

- **Self-Assessment:** Reflect on your skills, interests, and career goals. Consider how your priorities and aspirations may have evolved during your break.

- **Industry Insights:** Research your target industry or field to understand any changes, emerging trends, or new requirements. Stay informed about relevant developments.

- **Skill Refresh**: Identify skills that may need updating or refreshing to align with current industry standards. Consider taking courses or certifications as needed.

- **Resume and LinkedIn Profile:** Update your resume and LinkedIn profile to reflect your experiences during the career break. Highlight any relevant volunteer work, freelance projects, or skill development activities.

- **Networking:** Reconnect with former colleagues, mentors, and industry contacts. Attend networking events and online groups to rebuild your professional network.

- **Mindset Shift:** Embrace your career gap as a valuable experience that has contributed to your personal growth and skill set.

Actions to Take When Returning to the Workforce:

- **Set Clear Goals**: Define your career objectives and the type of work you're seeking. Having a specific direction will guide your job search.

- **Update Skills:** Invest in skill development or training if necessary to bridge any gaps in your qualifications. Consider online courses or workshops.

144

- **Volunteer or Freelance:** Engage in volunteer work, freelancing, or part-time projects to gain recent experience and references.

- Resume and Cover Letter: Tailor your application materials to emphasize your skills, achievements, and any relevant experiences gained during your career break.

- **Confidence Building:** Rebuild your confidence by participating in workshops, public speaking events, or courses that enhance your self-esteem.

- **Networking:** Attend industry events, conferences, and webinars to reconnect with professionals and stay updated on industry changes.

- **Mentorship:** Seek guidance from mentors or career coaches who can provide valuable insights and support.

- **Flexible Options:** Be open to exploring part-time, remote, or freelance opportunities as you transition back into the workforce.

- **Interview Preparation:** Practice your interview skills and prepare responses to common interview questions, including addressing your career break positively.

- **Work-Life Integration:** Consider how your return to work will affect your work-life balance and explore options that align with your priorities.

Returning to the workforce is an exciting chapter in your career journey. It's an opportunity to apply your skills and experiences to new challenges and opportunities. By taking proactive steps and maintaining a positive outlook, you can successfully resume your career and achieve your professional goals.

9.3 Virtual Interviews: Succeeding in the Digital Realm

In today's dynamic job market, virtual interviews have become increasingly prevalent. Whether you're transitioning to a new job, returning to the workforce, or exploring new career opportunities, mastering the art of virtual interviews is essential. This section equips you with the knowledge and strategies to excel in digital interviews.

Understanding the Significance of Virtual Interviews:

Virtual interviews offer several advantages, such as convenience, accessibility, and reduced time and cost associated with commuting. However, they also present unique challenges. Understanding these aspects is crucial:

- **Convenience:** Virtual interviews allow you to interview from the comfort of your home, eliminating the need for travel.

- **Technology**: Familiarity with video conferencing platforms and technical troubleshooting is essential.

- **Communication:** Effective communication through screens requires different skills than in-person interactions.

- **Non-Verbal Cues:** Interpreting and conveying non-verbal cues, such as body language and facial expressions, can be challenging in a virtual setting.

Actions to Excel in Virtual Interviews:

- **Technology Preparation:**

  - Familiarize yourself with the interview platform (e.g., Zoom, Skype, Microsoft Teams) and test your audio and video settings in advance.

  - Ensure a stable internet connection to avoid interruptions during the interview.

- **Professional Environment:**

  - Choose a quiet, well-lit space for your interview.

  - Remove distractions and inform household members about your interview to minimize interruptions.

- **Dress Appropriately:**

o   Dress professionally as you would for an in-person interview. Your attire reflects your seriousness about the opportunity.

- **Camera Etiquette:**

o   Position your camera at eye level to create a natural and engaging visual connection.

o   Maintain eye contact by looking into the camera when speaking, not at your screen.

- **Body Language:**

o   Practice positive body language, such as sitting up straight, smiling, and using hand gestures thoughtfully.

- **Communication Skills:**

o   Articulate your thoughts clearly and concisely.

o   Pause briefly after speaking to allow for potential audio delays.

- **Virtual Materials:**

o   Prepare digital copies of your resume, portfolio, or any documents you may need during the interview.

- **Practice Interviews:**

o   Conduct mock virtual interviews with a friend or career coach to refine your virtual communication skills.

- **Questions for the Interviewer:**

o   Prepare thoughtful questions about the company, role, and team to demonstrate your interest and engagement.

- **Follow-Up:**

o   Send a thank-you email promptly after the interview, expressing your gratitude and reiterating your interest in the position.

Mastering virtual interviews is not only about adapting to the digital realm but also about leveraging the advantages it offers. With the right preparation and techniques, you can make a lasting impression and effectively communicate your qualifications and enthusiasm to potential employers. Embrace the virtual interview as an opportunity to showcase your adaptability and readiness for the modern job market.

9.4 Mastering Panel Interviews: Winning Over the Committee

Panel interviews are a unique but increasingly common format in the hiring process. When facing a committee of interviewers, you need to navigate the dynamics, personalities, and questions effectively. This section provides you with insights and strategies to excel in panel interviews and make a lasting impression on the entire committee.

Understanding Panel Interviews:

- **Multiple Perspectives:** Panel interviews involve multiple interviewers, each representing a different aspect of the company or team. Their questions may vary to assess various skills and qualities.

- **Collaborative Decision-Making:** Panelists often collaborate to evaluate candidates and make informed decisions. Your responses and interactions impact each panelist's perception.

- **Diverse Questions:** Expect a wide range of questions, from technical and situational to behavioral and cultural fit inquiries.

- **Dynamic Interactions:** Panel interviews require you to manage interactions with multiple interviewers simultaneously, which can be challenging.

Actions to Excel in Panel Interviews:

- **Preparation:**

  o   Research each panelist's role and background to understand their perspectives and priorities.

  o   Anticipate diverse questions and practice responses that showcase your skills and experiences.

- **Engagement:**

  o Address each panelist when responding to their questions, maintaining eye contact and active listening.

  o Aim to create a rapport with the entire panel, demonstrating your ability to collaborate.

- **Structure Your Responses:**

  o Deliver concise, well-structured answers that provide specific examples and solutions.

  o Use the STAR (Situation, Task, Action, Result) method for behavioral questions to ensure clarity.

- **Balance Addressing All Panelists:**

  o Ensure that you engage with all panelists, even if one person asks a question. Acknowledge their interest and perspectives.

- **Adaptability:**

-     Be prepared to pivot smoothly between topics and respond to follow-up questions from different panelists.

- **Questions for the Committee:**

  ○   Prepare questions that show your interest in the company's mission, team dynamics, and your potential role in achieving organizational goals.

- **Confidence and Poise:**

  ○   Maintain composure under pressure and exude confidence in your abilities.

- **Thank the Entire Panel:**

  ○   After the interview, send personalized thank-you emails to each panelist, expressing your appreciation for their time and insights.

Panel interviews offer a comprehensive evaluation process that can provide valuable insights into your fit for the role and organization. By mastering the art of panel interviews and effectively engaging with all committee members, you increase your chances of making

a positive impression and securing your desired position.

Remember that each interaction is an opportunity to showcase your

skills, experiences, and readiness to contribute to the team's

success.

Chapter 10: Post-Interview Excellence

In this chapter, you will continue your journey beyond interviews. Craft impeccable thank-you notes, juggle multiple job offers, make the final decision, and master background checks and references.

10.1 Crafting Impeccable Thank-You Notes

The interview doesn't end when you walk out of the company's door or log off from the virtual meeting platform. In fact, one of the most crucial aspects of the post-interview process is crafting a thoughtful and impeccable thank-you note.

Why Are Thank-You Notes Important?

A well-crafted thank-you note serves several purposes:

- **Expressing Gratitude**: First and foremost, it's an opportunity to express your appreciation for the interviewers' time and consideration. This simple gesture reflects your professionalism and manners.

- **Reiterating Interest:** A thank-you note allows you to reiterate your enthusiasm for the position and the company. It reminds the interviewers of your strong interest in the role.

- **Highlighting Key Points:** You can use the note to highlight key points from the interview that you want to emphasize. This is a chance to reinforce the skills, experiences, and qualities that make you a great fit for the job.

- **Addressing Missed Points:** If you feel you missed mentioning something important during the interview, you can include it in the thank-you note. It's an opportunity to provide any additional information that might strengthen your candidacy.

How to Craft the Perfect Thank-You Note

- **Send It Promptly:** Timing matters. Ideally, send your thank-you note within 24 hours of the interview. It demonstrates your eagerness and attention to detail.

- **Personalize Each Note:** Avoid sending a generic thank-you note to everyone you interviewed with. Personalize each message, referring to specific points of discussion or unique aspects of your conversation.

- **Express Genuine Appreciation:** Start by expressing your gratitude for the opportunity to interview. A simple "Thank you for taking the time to meet with me" is a good beginning.

- **Reiterate Your Interest:** Mention your continued interest in the position and why you believe it's the right fit for you. Highlight a particular aspect of the company or role that excites you.

- **Highlight Key Qualities:** Reinforce the key qualifications and skills that make you a strong candidate. Use specific examples from the interview to back up your claims.

- **Address Concerns**: If there were any concerns or doubts raised during the interview, use the thank-you note as a chance to address them or provide additional context.

- **Maintain Professionalism:** Keep the tone of your thank-you note professional and positive. Avoid negative comments or criticism of any kind.

- **Keep It Concise:** A thank-you note should be brief and to the point. Aim for no more than a few paragraphs.

- **Proofread Carefully:** Just like your resume, your thank-you note should be free of spelling and grammatical errors. Take the time to proofread before hitting send.

A Lasting Impression

In the competitive world of job interviews, it's the small details that can set you apart. Crafting impeccable thank-you notes is one of those details. These notes not only express your gratitude but also provide an additional opportunity to demonstrate your suitability for the position. Don't underestimate the power of this simple yet effective post-interview practice.

10.2 Juggling Multiple Job Offers

Congratulations! You've successfully navigated through the interview process and found yourself in a fortunate position – multiple job offers on the table. This chapter will guide you through the delicate art of managing and deciding between multiple job offers, ensuring that you make the right choice for your career.

The Dilemma of Choice

Having multiple job offers is undoubtedly a testament to your skills and qualifications, but it can also be overwhelming. The decisions you make at this stage can significantly impact your career path, job satisfaction, and overall happiness. Here's how to approach the dilemma of choice:

- **Assess Your Priorities:**

o   Reflect on your career goals and personal priorities. What matters most to you – salary, job location, company culture, career growth opportunities, or work-life balance?

o   Create a list of your top priorities and rank them to understand what aspects of a job are non-negotiable for you.

- **Compare Offers Objectively:**

o   Gather all the necessary information about each job offer, including compensation packages, benefits, job responsibilities, and company culture.

o   Create a spreadsheet or list to compare these aspects across offers, making it easier to see the pros and cons of each position.

- **Seek Clarifications:**

o   If you have questions or concerns about any offer, don't hesitate to reach out to the respective employers.

Seeking clarification can help you make an informed decision.

- **Consider Long-Term Growth:**

  o   Think beyond immediate benefits. Consider which job offers the most potential for long-term career growth and development.

  o   Assess the company's reputation, opportunities for advancement, and alignment with your career aspirations.

- **Cultural Fit:**

  o   Evaluate how well you fit into the company culture. A harmonious work environment can significantly impact your job satisfaction.

  o   Consider your interactions with potential colleagues during the interview process.

- **Consult Trusted Advisors:**

o   Seek advice from mentors, career coaches, or

trusted friends who can provide valuable insights and an

outside perspective on your options.

- **Negotiation:**

o   If you have a clear top choice, but it falls short in

certain areas, consider negotiating with the employer.

Sometimes, they may be willing to adjust certain aspects of

the offer to meet your needs.

- **Time Constraints:**

o   Be mindful of any time constraints. Some

employers may require a quick decision, so manage your

time wisely to avoid missing out on opportunities.

Making the Decision

Ultimately, the key to juggling multiple job offers lies in aligning

your choice with your career goals and personal values. It's not just about finding a job; it's about finding the right job for you. Here are some actionable steps to help you make that decision:

- **Trust Your Instincts:**
  - Listen to your gut feeling. Sometimes, your intuition can guide you toward the right choice.
  - Visualize yourself in each role and consider which one excites you the most.

- **Balance Your Priorities:**
  - Weigh the importance of each priority against the others. It may not be possible to have everything you want, so prioritize accordingly.

- **Be Honest with Employers:**
  - If you need more time to make a decision or if you've accepted another offer, communicate this honestly with the respective employers. It's essential to maintain professionalism throughout the process.

- **Accept Gracefully:**

o Once you've made your decision, accept the job offer gracefully. Send a well-crafted acceptance letter and express your enthusiasm for joining the organization.

- **Decline Professionally:**
  o For the offers you're declining, send polite and appreciative rejection letters. You never know when your paths may cross again in the future.

Remember that while multiple job offers can be a delightful challenge, it's a privilege that reflects your qualifications and efforts. Approach the decision-making process with careful consideration, and you'll be well on your way to a successful and fulfilling career journey.

10.3 Making the Final Decision

You've navigated the interview process, received multiple job offers, and diligently assessed your priorities. Now, you stand at the crossroads, ready to make one of the most crucial decisions in your career – selecting the job that aligns with your goals, values, and aspirations. In this chapter, we'll delve into the art of making the final decision and offer guidance on how to choose the path that leads you to professional fulfillment.

Understanding the Weight of the Decision

Choosing the right job is not merely about securing employment; it's about setting the trajectory for your future. The decisions you make can influence your career growth, job satisfaction, and overall well-being. Here's how to approach this pivotal moment:

- **Reflect on Your Priorities:**

o   Revisit the list of priorities you established earlier in your job search. Which aspects of a job matter most to you?

o   Consider your long-term career goals and how each job offer aligns with them.

- **Reevaluate Your Top Choice:**

    o   If you have a front-runner among your job offers, scrutinize it once more. Are there any aspects you may have overlooked?

    o   Ensure that your decision isn't based solely on immediate gratification but takes into account your long-term vision.

- **Seek Feedback:**

    o   Consult with mentors, career advisors, or trusted friends who can provide valuable insights. An outside perspective can help you see the bigger picture.

    o   Discuss your options and concerns openly to gain clarity.

- **Visualize Your Future:**

o   Imagine yourself in each role, considering the day-to-day responsibilities, company culture, and work environment.

o   Picture the impact of your choice on your personal life and overall career trajectory.

- **Conduct a SWOT Analysis:**

    o   Perform a SWOT (Strengths, Weaknesses, Opportunities, Threats) analysis for each job offer. Evaluate the strengths and weaknesses of each role, the opportunities they present, and the potential challenges.

    o   This structured approach can provide a clearer perspective on your options.

- **Gather Additional Information:**

    o   If you still have questions or doubts about any offer, reach out to the employers for clarification. It's essential to have all the information you need to make an informed choice.

The Power of Intuition and Gut Feeling

While data and analysis are crucial, don't underestimate the power of intuition. Your gut feeling can often guide you toward the right decision. If one opportunity excites you more than the others and aligns with your values, it's a strong indicator that it may be the right choice.

Taking the Leap

Once you've made your decision, it's time to take the leap and embrace your chosen path. Here are some actionable steps:

- **Accept the Offer:**
  - Write a gracious acceptance letter to the employer of your chosen job. Express your enthusiasm and commitment to the role.
  - Be prompt in your response to demonstrate professionalism.

- **Decline with Gratitude:**

  o   Notify the employers of the offers you're declining with polite and appreciative rejection letters. Maintain a positive relationship for potential future interactions.

- **Set Your Goals:**

  o   Establish clear and achievable short-term and long-term career goals that align with your new job. Create a roadmap for your professional development.

- **Network and Connect:**

  o   Start building relationships within your new organization. Connect with colleagues, supervisors, and mentors who can support your growth.

- **Continual Evaluation:**

  o   Regularly assess your career path to ensure it remains aligned with your goals. Be open to reassessing your priorities and making adjustments when necessary.

Conclusion: The Path Ahead

Making the final decision is both exhilarating and daunting. It signifies the beginning of a new chapter in your career journey. Remember that your choice reflects your aspirations, values, and potential. Embrace it wholeheartedly, and trust that your decision will lead you toward personal and professional fulfillment. The path ahead is filled with opportunities for growth, learning, and success. Congratulations on reaching this milestone in your career!

10.4 Navigating Background Checks and References

As you approach the final stages of securing your dream job, there's one last hurdle to clear – background checks and references. Employers conduct these checks to verify the information you've provided, assess your suitability for the role, and ensure a seamless transition into their organization. In this chapter, we'll explore the intricacies of this essential step and guide you through the process of navigating background checks and references with confidence.

Understanding Background Checks

Background checks are a standard part of the hiring process for many organizations. They typically involve verifying your employment history, educational credentials, criminal record, and sometimes your credit history. Here's what you need to know:

- **Consent and Authorization:**
    - Before conducting a background check, employers must obtain your written consent. Read the authorization form carefully, and ensure you provide accurate information.

- **Employment Verification:**
    - Employers will contact your previous workplaces to confirm your job titles, dates of employment, salary

history, and reasons for leaving. Ensure your resume aligns with this information.

- **Educational Verification:**

  o Your educational credentials, such as degrees and certifications, will be verified with the respective institutions. Be truthful about your academic achievements.

- **Criminal Background Check:**

  o In some industries, a criminal background check is required. Be transparent about any past convictions and provide context if necessary.

- **Credit History Check:**

  o Some positions, particularly those involving financial responsibilities, may require a credit history check. Maintain good financial practices and address any discrepancies proactively.

- **Social Media and Online Presence:**

  o Employers may review your online presence, including social media profiles, to gauge your professionalism and alignment with their company values. Ensure your online persona is in line with your desired image.

Preparing Your References

References play a crucial role in the hiring process, providing employers with insights into your character, work ethic, and qualifications. Here's how to prepare your references effectively:

- **Choose Wisely:**
  - Select references who can speak to your skills, accomplishments, and character. Former supervisors, colleagues, or mentors who know your work well are excellent choices.

- **Request Permission:**
  - Always ask for permission before listing someone as a reference. Explain the role you're applying for and provide them with any necessary information.

- **Keep Them Informed:**

  o Share your current resume, the job description, and
  key points you'd like them to emphasize when contacted by
  the employer.

- **Maintain a Reference List:**

  o Create a reference list that includes the individual's
  name, title, company, contact information, and the nature of
  your professional relationship.

- **Follow Up:**

  o Once you've provided references, follow up with
  them to inform them when they might be contacted.
  Express your gratitude for their support.

Dealing with Challenges

Occasionally, discrepancies or challenges may arise during
background checks or reference checks. Here's how to handle
them:

- **Address Discrepancies:**

  o   If a discrepancy is identified during the background check, be prepared to explain it honestly. Transparency is essential in maintaining trust.

- **Communicate with References:**

  o   Keep your references informed of any potential calls or emails they may receive. Ensure they are available and prepared to respond promptly.

- **Be Professional:**

  o   Maintain professionalism throughout the process. Even if you face challenges, a composed and respectful demeanor will reflect positively on you.

Conclusion: The Final Step

Navigating background checks and references is the last step before stepping into your new role. Embrace this process as an opportunity to showcase your honesty, integrity, and professionalism. By maintaining clear communication, choosing your references thoughtfully, and addressing any challenges with grace, you'll navigate this final hurdle successfully. Soon, you'll be embarking on an exciting journey in your new job, confident that you've left no stone unturned in securing your dream position.

Chapter 11: The Future of Interviews

In this chapter, you will Peer into the future of interviews. Explore the impact of technological advancements, master virtual interviews, delve into AI-driven interviews, and stay relevant in a changing landscape.

11.1 Technological Advancements and Interviews

In this chapter, we'll explore the ever-evolving landscape of job interviews in the face of technological advancements. We'll examine the changes that technology has brought to interviews and discuss what actions interviewers should consider in this tech-driven era.

The Changing Landscape of Interviews

The interview process is undergoing a significant transformation due to technological advancements. Here are some key trends and technological developments that are reshaping interviews:

- **Virtual Reality (VR) and Augmented Reality (AR):** VR and AR technologies are changing the way interviews are conducted. Candidates can now engage in immersive virtual interviews, where they interact with virtual environments or even holographic interviewers.

- **Artificial Intelligence (AI) and Chatbots:** AI-powered chatbots are increasingly being utilized for initial candidate screenings. These bots can conduct text-based interviews, pose predefined questions, and analyze responses to identify suitable candidates.

- **Video Interviews:** Video interviews, whether prerecorded or live, have become commonplace. AI algorithms can analyze candidates' facial expressions, tone of voice, and body language to provide insights into their suitability for the role.

- **Gamification:** Some organizations are incorporating gamification elements into interviews. Candidates may be asked to complete job-related challenges or games to assess their skills and problem-solving abilities.

- **Remote Work and Globalization:** The rise of remote work has made it common for candidates to interview for positions in different geographic locations. Video conferencing tools and collaboration platforms facilitate these global interviews.

- **Behavioral Analysis:** AI-driven tools can analyze candidates' writing samples, social media profiles, or recorded responses to predict their cultural fit and personality traits.

Actions for Interviewers

In this tech-driven era, interviewers must adapt to these technological advancements to ensure effective and fair interview processes. Here's what interviewers should consider:

- **Tech Proficiency:** Familiarize yourself with the interview technology being used, such as video conferencing platforms and AI screening tools. Ensure that you can effectively operate these platforms to provide a seamless experience for candidates.

- **Virtual Etiquette:** When conducting virtual interviews, pay attention to your background, lighting, and camera angles. Dress professionally and create a conducive virtual environment that reflects your organization's image.

- **AI Interaction:** If using AI or chatbots for initial screenings, design clear and relevant questions for candidates. Be prepared to interpret responses within the context of the job requirements.

- **Adaptability:** Be ready to conduct interviews in various formats, including traditional, video, and gamified interviews. Tailor your questions and evaluation criteria to align with the specific interview format.

- **Global Sensitivity:** When interviewing candidates from different regions, consider cultural differences in communication styles and expectations. Foster inclusivity and respect for diversity in the interview process.

- **Data Security:** Safeguard candidate data and ensure compliance with privacy regulations. Communicate clearly with candidates about data usage and storage practices.

- **Continuous Learning:** Stay updated on emerging interview technologies and best practices. Invest in training and development to effectively leverage these tools.

The future of interviews offers exciting possibilities, but it also requires interviewers to adapt and stay informed. Embrace technology, foster a candidate-centric approach, and uphold professionalism in the interview process. By doing so, you can effectively harness the benefits of technological advancements while maintaining a fair and equitable interview experience for all candidates.

11.2 Mastering Virtual Interviews

In recent years, the landscape of job interviews has evolved significantly, with virtual interviews becoming increasingly prevalent. Whether you're interviewing for remote positions, making a long-distance career change, or adapting to the changing times, mastering virtual interviews is essential in today's job market. This chapter explores the intricacies of virtual interviews and equips you with the knowledge and skills to excel in this digital realm.

Understanding Virtual Interviews

Virtual interviews come in various formats, such as video interviews, phone interviews, and web-based assessments. Here's what you need to know about each type:

- **Video Interviews:** Video interviews closely resemble traditional face-to-face interviews but are conducted using video conferencing platforms like Zoom, Skype, or Microsoft Teams. They allow for real-time interaction with the interviewer.

- **Phone Interviews:** Phone interviews are conducted over the phone and typically focus on screening candidates or gathering initial information. While they may seem less formal, they are just as crucial in the interview process.

- **Web-Based Assessments:** Some employers use web-based platforms to assess candidates' skills and abilities through online tests, coding challenges, or simulations. These assessments can be a significant part of the interview process, especially for technical roles.

Preparing for Virtual Interviews

Mastering virtual interviews requires careful preparation and consideration of unique challenges. Here are some key aspects to focus on:

- **Technical Readiness:** Ensure you have a stable internet connection, a working camera, and clear audio. Familiarize yourself with the video conferencing platform you'll be using.
- **Environment:**

  o Choose a quiet, well-lit space for your interview. Remove distractions and ensure your background is professional and uncluttered.

- **Attire:**

o Dress professionally from head to toe, even if you think the interviewer will only see the upper half of your body. Feeling put-together can boost your confidence.

- **Practice:**

  o Conduct mock virtual interviews with a friend or family member to get comfortable with the technology and practice answering questions.

- **Body Language:** Maintain eye contact by looking into the camera, not at your screen. Sit up straight and use gestures sparingly to convey confidence and engagement.

During the Virtual Interview

During the actual virtual interview, remember these essential tips:

- **Engagement:** Show your enthusiasm and interest by actively participating in the conversation. Listen carefully and ask relevant questions.

- **Eye Contact:** Focus on the camera when speaking, not the interviewer's image on your screen. This creates the illusion of eye contact.

- **Clear Communication:** Speak clearly and at a moderate pace. Ensure your responses are concise and relevant to the questions asked.

- **Technology Backup:** Have a backup device or phone ready in case of technical issues. Communicate proactively with the interviewer if you encounter any problems.

Follow-Up and Thank-You Notes

After a virtual interview, send a thank-you email expressing your appreciation for the opportunity. Reiterate your interest in the position and briefly summarize why you're a great fit. This step is just as crucial in the virtual world as it is in traditional interviews.

Conclusion: Navigating the Digital Frontier

Mastering virtual interviews is a valuable skill in today's job market. By understanding the nuances of different virtual interview formats, preparing meticulously, and showcasing your professionalism and engagement during the interview, you'll be well-equipped to navigate the digital frontier of job interviews. Embrace this evolution in the interview process as an opportunity to shine, and you'll be one step closer to landing your dream job in the digital age.

11.3 AI-Driven Interviews: What Lies Ahead?

The world of job interviews is on the brink of another transformation as artificial intelligence (AI) continues to revolutionize various industries, including hiring. In this chapter, we'll explore the emergence of AI-driven interviews, how they are changing the way candidates are assessed, and what the future holds in this rapidly evolving landscape.

The Role of AI in Interviews

AI-driven interviews encompass a range of technologies and applications, each designed to streamline the interview process. Here are some key aspects of AI's role:

- **Resume Screening:**

  - AI algorithms are used to scan and evaluate resumes, identifying qualified candidates based on predefined criteria.

- **Chatbots and Virtual Assistants:** Chatbots and virtual assistants can conduct initial interviews with candidates, asking scripted questions and providing information about the role and company.

- **Video Interviews:** AI can analyze video interviews, assessing candidates' facial expressions, tone of voice, and language to gauge their suitability for the role.

- **Predictive Analytics:** AI can analyze data from previous hires to predict which candidates are most likely to succeed in a particular role.

- **Skill Assessment:** AI platforms can assess candidates' technical skills through online tests and simulations, providing objective evaluations.

Preparing for AI-Driven Interviews

As AI becomes more integrated into the interview process, candidates must adapt to this new reality. Here's how to prepare:

- **Understand AI Tools:** Familiarize yourself with the AI tools commonly used in hiring processes. Research the technology and its capabilities.

- **Optimize Your Resume:** Craft your resume to be AI-friendly by including relevant keywords and formatting that AI systems can easily parse.

- **Practice Video Interviews:** Practice video interviews to become comfortable with the technology. Pay attention to your body language and tone of voice.

- **Be Concise:** When answering AI-generated questions, be concise and to the point. Avoid rambling or providing excessive information.

- **Embrace Skill Development:** Continuously improve your skills, as AI often assesses technical competencies. Consider online courses and certifications.

The Ethical Considerations of AI Interviews

With the integration of AI, ethical considerations become paramount. Issues related to bias, privacy, and transparency need to be addressed by both employers and AI developers. As a candidate, it's essential to be aware of your rights and question any AI-driven processes that raise ethical concerns.

The Future of AI-Driven Interviews

The future of AI-driven interviews is promising but also presents challenges. As AI algorithms become more sophisticated, they will offer increasingly accurate assessments of candidates. However, striking a balance between automation and human judgment will remain a critical challenge. Job seekers will need to adapt to this evolving landscape, emphasizing their unique qualities and abilities that AI cannot measure.

Conclusion: Navigating the AI Frontier

AI-driven interviews represent the next frontier in the world of job interviews. While they bring unprecedented efficiency and objectivity, they also raise ethical and practical questions. By understanding the role of AI, preparing effectively, and staying attuned to industry developments, candidates can navigate this evolving landscape and continue their journey toward interview excellence in the digital age.

11.4 Staying Relevant in the Changing Interview Landscape

The world of job interviews is constantly evolving, influenced by technological advancements, shifts in industry trends, and changes in employer preferences. In this chapter, we'll explore the importance of staying relevant in the ever-changing interview landscape and how you can adapt to secure your dream job.

Embracing Lifelong Learning

One of the keys to staying relevant in the interview landscape is embracing the concept of lifelong learning. This means continuously updating your knowledge and skills to keep pace with industry developments. Here's how you can do it:

- **Stay Informed:** Regularly read industry publications, blogs, and news to stay updated on the latest trends, technologies, and best practices.

- **Take Online Courses:** Enroll in online courses, webinars, and workshops to acquire new skills or enhance existing ones. Platforms like Coursera, edX, and LinkedIn Learning offer a wealth of opportunities.

- **Attend Conferences and Seminars:** Participate in industry-specific conferences and seminars. These events provide valuable insights, networking opportunities, and exposure to emerging trends.

- **Join Professional Associations:** Become a member of professional associations related to your field. These organizations often offer resources, certifications, and networking events.

- **Seek Mentoring:** Find a mentor or career coach who can guide you in your professional development journey. They can provide valuable advice and help you set goals.

Adapting to Remote Work Trends

The COVID-19 pandemic accelerated the adoption of remote work. As a result, many interviews and job roles shifted to a remote format. To stay relevant in this changing landscape:

- **Enhance Your Digital Literacy:** Improve your proficiency in digital tools and platforms commonly used in remote work, such as video conferencing, project management software, and collaboration tools.

- **Showcase Remote Work Skills:** Highlight your ability to work independently, manage your time effectively, and communicate remotely on your resume and during interviews.

- **Develop Soft Skills:** Soft skills like adaptability, communication, and problem-solving become even more crucial in a remote work environment.

- **Create a Professional Home Office:** Set up a dedicated and professional workspace at home for remote interviews and work. Ensure a clutter-free and well-lit environment.

The Role of Networking

Networking remains a powerful tool in the job search process. Building and maintaining a professional network can help you stay informed about job opportunities and industry developments.

- **Connect on LinkedIn:** Utilize LinkedIn to connect with professionals in your industry, join relevant groups, and follow thought leaders.
- **Attend Virtual Networking Events:** Participate in virtual networking events, webinars, and online meetups to expand your professional network.
- **Seek Informational Interviews:** Conduct informational interviews with professionals in your field to gather insights and advice.

- **Engage in Alumni Networks:** Leverage alumni networks from your educational institutions to connect with fellow graduates.

Conclusion: Embracing Change for Success

In a rapidly changing interview landscape, the ability to adapt, learn, and network is essential. By embracing lifelong learning, adapting to remote work trends, and nurturing your professional network, you can stay relevant and increase your chances of securing the job you desire. Remember that the interview landscape may evolve, but your commitment to growth and improvement will remain a constant asset.

Chapter 12. Sample Behavioral Questions and Answers

Apply your knowledge with real-world examples. Practice answering behavioral questions and develop strategies for showcasing your skills effectively.

12.1 Leadership and Teamwork:

Sample Question 1: Tell me about a time when you had to work under tight deadlines. How did you prioritize your tasks and ensure timely completion?

Step 1: Understand the Situation. Begin your response by setting the stage. Provide context about the specific situation or project where you faced tight deadlines. Make sure to include the following:

- The company or organization you were working for.

- The project, task, or assignment involved.

- The tight deadline or time constraints you were under.

Sample Response (Situation): *"In my previous role as a marketing coordinator at XYZ Company, we were tasked with launching a new product campaign for a major client. The client had requested an aggressive timeline, and we had just three weeks to develop and execute the entire campaign."*

Step 2: Describe Your Actions After providing context, explain the actions you took to address the tight deadlines. Focus on how you prioritized tasks and ensured timely completion. Include details such as:

- The specific steps you took to plan and organize your work.

- Any strategies you used to manage your time effectively?

- How did you communicate with team members or stakeholders?

Sample Response (Actions): *"To manage the tight deadlines, I immediately convened a project kickoff meeting with our team to outline the campaign's objectives, roles, and responsibilities. We created a detailed project plan with clear milestones and deadlines. I prioritized tasks based on their criticality to the campaign's success and assigned team members accordingly. We also leveraged project management software to track progress in real time, which helped us stay on course."*

Step 3: Highlight the Results. Conclude your response by describing the positive outcome or results of your actions. Mention how you were able to meet or exceed the tight deadlines and the impact it had on the project or organization. Emphasize any specific achievements, such as meeting client expectations or delivering high-quality work.

Sample Response (Results): *"As a result of our efforts, we not only met the client's tight deadline but also exceeded their expectations. The campaign was launched successfully and* *generated a 20% increase in sales for the client within the first*

month. Our ability to work under pressure and deliver exceptional

results strengthened our client relationships and showcased our

team's dedication to meeting challenging deadlines."

Key Tips:

• Use the STAR method (Situation, Task, Action, Result) to structure your response effectively.

• Be concise and focus on the most relevant details.

• Highlight any leadership or teamwork skills you employed.

• Showcase your ability to handle high-pressure situations and meet deadlines.

Sample Question 2: Describe a situation where you had to resolve a conflict within your team or with a colleague. What approach did you take, and what was the outcome?

Step 1: Set the Scene Begin your response by providing context and background information about the situation where the conflict arose. Include the following details:

- The company or organization you were working for.

- The team or colleague involved in the conflict.

- The nature of the conflict or the specific issue that triggered it.

Sample Response (Situation): *"In my previous role as a project manager at ABC Corporation, I was leading a cross-functional team working on a critical project. There was a conflict between two team members, Sarah and John, regarding the allocation of project tasks. Both believed they should be responsible for a key component, and this disagreement was affecting team dynamics and project progress."*

Step 2: Describe Your Actions. Next, explain the actions you took to address and resolve the conflict. Focus on the specific steps you followed and your approach to resolving the issue. Highlight the following aspects:

- How you initiated the conflict resolution process.

- The strategies you employed to facilitate communication and understanding.

- Any compromise, negotiation, or mediation efforts you made.

Sample Response (Actions): *"To address the conflict, I first scheduled a private meeting with both Sarah and John to understand their perspectives. I actively listened to their concerns and validated their viewpoints. I emphasized the importance of teamwork and the project's success. Next, I organized a team meeting where I facilitated an open and constructive discussion. During the meeting, I encouraged both Sarah and John to express their ideas and concerns, and I mediated the conversation to ensure it remained respectful and focused on solutions."*

Step 3: Highlight the Results. Conclude your response by discussing the outcome of your conflict resolution efforts. Describe how your actions led to a resolution and what positive impact it had on the team or project. Mention any changes in team dynamics or the working relationship between those involved.

Sample Response (Results): *"As a result of our conflict resolution efforts, Sarah and John were able to reach a mutual understanding and agreement on the task allocation. They recognized each other's strengths and contributions to the project. This resolution led to improved collaboration within the team, and we saw a significant boost in productivity. Both team members became more engaged and motivated to work together effectively, and we successfully met our project milestones."*

Key Tips:

• Use the STAR method (Situation, Task, Action, Result) to structure your response effectively.

- Highlight your interpersonal and communication skills.

- Emphasize your ability to mediate and facilitate productive discussions.

- Showcase your commitment to teamwork and problem-solving.

Sample Question 3: Can you share an example of a project or task that required you to showcase your leadership skills? How did you motivate and lead your team to success?

Step 1: Set the Scene Begin your response by providing context and background information about the project or task where you demonstrated your leadership skills. Include the following details:

- The company, organization, or team you were part of.

- The nature of the project or task.

- The challenges or goals associated with it.

Sample Response (Situation): *"In my previous role as a project manager at XYZ Company, I was assigned to lead a critical project aimed at developing a new product line. The project was challenging because it had tight deadlines, a cross-functional team, and a need for innovative solutions to stay competitive in the market."*

Step 2: Describe Your Actions. Next, explain the specific actions you took to lead and motivate your team effectively. Highlight the leadership strategies you employed and how you managed the project's challenges. Include the following aspects:

- How you inspired and motivated team members.

- The strategies you used to delegate tasks and responsibilities.

- Any obstacles you encountered and how you overcame them.

Sample Response (Actions): *"To ensure the project's success, I focused on creating a collaborative and motivated team environment. I started by clearly defining roles and responsibilities for each team member, aligning their strengths with specific project tasks. I held regular team meetings to communicate our goals, progress, and expectations.*

Additionally, I encouraged open communication and idea-sharing within the team, ensuring that everyone's input was valued. When we faced challenges, I facilitated brainstorming sessions to find innovative solutions. I also provided consistent feedback and recognition to team members, acknowledging their contributions and reinforcing a positive work atmosphere."

Step 3: Highlight the Results. Conclude your response by discussing the outcomes and achievements resulting from your leadership efforts. Describe how your leadership skills positively influenced the project's success and the team's performance.

Mention any specific results, improvements, or milestones achieved.

Sample Response (Results): *"As a result of our collaborative efforts and effective leadership, our team not only met but exceeded project milestones and deadlines. We successfully launched the new product line ahead of schedule, which resulted in a significant increase in market share and revenue. Team morale was at an all-time high, and the project's success was celebrated throughout the organization. This experience reinforced the importance of leadership, teamwork, and motivation in achieving outstanding results."*

Key Tips:

- Use the STAR method (Situation, Task, Action, Result) to structure your response effectively.

- Highlight your leadership qualities, including communication, delegation, motivation, and problem-solving.

- Provide specific examples of how you addressed challenges or obstacles.

- Showcase your ability to inspire and lead a team toward success.

12.2 Adaptability and Change Management:

Sample Question 1: Tell me about a time when you had to adapt to a major change at work, such as a new process or technology. How did you approach the change, and what was the result?

Step 1: Set the Scene Begin your response by providing context and background information about the situation in which you had to adapt to a major change at work. Include the following details:

- The company or organization where this occurred.

- The nature of the change such as the introduction of a new process or technology.

- The challenges or issues associated with this change.

Sample Response (Situation): *"In my previous role at ABC Corporation, our department underwent a significant change when the company decided to implement a new project management software. This transition was essential to improve efficiency and streamline our project workflows, but it posed a challenge due to the learning curve associated with the new technology."*

Step 2: Describe Your Actions. Next, explain the specific actions you took to adapt to the major change effectively. Highlight the strategies and steps you employed to navigate the transition smoothly. Include the following aspects:

- How did you approach the change, including any proactive measures?

- Steps you took to acquire new skills or knowledge.

- Any obstacles or difficulties you encountered during the adaptation process.

Sample Response (Actions): *"To approach this change, I knew it was crucial to be proactive. I began by attending training sessions and workshops organized by our IT department to familiarize myself with the new project management software. I also reached out to colleagues who were already proficient in using the software to seek guidance and best practices.*

Additionally, I created a personal learning plan that included online tutorials, self-paced modules, and daily practice. I set aside dedicated time each day to explore the software's features and functionalities, ensuring that I was making steady progress."

Step 3: Highlight the Results. Conclude your response by discussing the outcomes and results of your efforts to adapt to the major change. Describe how your approach positively impacted your work, productivity, or the overall effectiveness of the new process or technology.

Sample Response (Results): *"As a result of my proactive approach and dedication to adapting to the new software, I quickly*

211

became proficient in its use. This not only enhanced my personal productivity but also contributed to the department's overall efficiency. I was able to help colleagues who were still transitioning, providing guidance and support.

The successful adoption of the new project management software led to improved project tracking, reduced errors, and streamlined communication within our team. Our projects were completed more efficiently, and we met deadlines with greater consistency."

Key Tips:

• Structure your response using the STAR method (Situation, Task, Action, Result).

• Emphasize your adaptability, problem-solving, and commitment to overcoming challenges.

• Be specific about the actions you took and the skills you acquired during the adaptation process.

- Highlight the positive impact of your adaptation on your work and the organization.

Sample Question 2: Give me an example of a challenging problem you faced at work. How did you go about identifying the problem, and what steps did you take to find a solution?

Step 1: Set the Scene Begin your response by providing context and background information about the challenging problem you encountered at work. Include the following details:

- The company or organization where this occurred.

- The nature of the problem, including its significance and impact.

- The specific circumstances surrounding the problem.

Sample Response (Situation): *"In my previous role at XYZ Company, we faced a significant challenge related to a declining customer satisfaction rate. Our customer feedback indicated that our response times to customer inquiries and complaints were slower than industry standards, resulting in customer frustration and potential business loss. It was clear that we needed to address this issue urgently."*

Step 2: Describe Your Actions. Next, explain the specific actions you took to identify and address the challenging problem effectively. Highlight the strategies and steps you employed to tackle the issue. Include the following aspects:

• How did you identify the problem and the methods or tools used?

• The steps you took to analyze and gather relevant data or information.

• Any obstacles or complexities you encountered during the problem-solving process.

Sample Response (Actions): *"To address this challenge, I initiated a comprehensive review of our customer service operations. I began by collecting and analyzing data on response times, customer complaints, and service request volumes. This data allowed me to identify patterns and bottlenecks in our processes.*

I also conducted interviews with our customer service team to gain insights into their workflows and challenges. This qualitative information complemented the quantitative data and provided a holistic view of the problem. Additionally, I researched industry best practices to identify potential solutions."

Step 3: Highlight the Results. Conclude your response by discussing the outcomes and results of your efforts to address the challenging problem. Describe how your approach led to a solution and the positive impact it had on the organization or the situation.

Sample Response (Results): *"As a result of the actions I took, we were able to pinpoint the root causes of the slow response times and customer dissatisfaction. With a clear understanding of the*

215

problem, I worked with the customer service team to implement

process improvements and workflow optimizations.

These changes resulted in a 30% reduction in response times

within two months, leading to a significant improvement in

customer satisfaction scores. We also saw a decrease in customer

complaints and an increase in customer retention rates.

Ultimately, our efforts not only resolved the immediate problem

but also enhanced our overall customer service capabilities."

Key Tips:

• Structure your response using the STAR method (Situation, Task, Action, Result).

• Emphasize your problem-solving skills, analytical abilities, and initiative.

• Be specific about the actions you took and the impact of your solution.

- Highlight the positive outcomes and benefits for the organization or team.

Sample Question 3: Share a situation where you had to handle a dissatisfied customer or client. How did you address their concerns and ensure their satisfaction?

Step 1: Set the Scene. Start by providing context and background information about the situation where you had to deal with a dissatisfied customer or client. Include the following details:

- The company or organization where this occurred.

- The nature of the customer's concern or dissatisfaction.

- Any specific circumstances surrounding the interaction.

Sample Response (Situation): *"In my previous role at ABC Corporation, I encountered a situation where a long-standing client expressed deep dissatisfaction with a recent project we had delivered. The client had raised concerns about the project's quality, missed deadlines, and a lack of communication during the* *process. Their dissatisfaction was evident through emails and phone calls expressing frustration."*

Step 2: Describe Your Actions. Explain the specific actions you took to address the dissatisfied customer's concerns and ensure their satisfaction. Highlight the strategies and steps you employed to resolve the issue. Include the following aspects:

• How you listened to the customer's concerns and empathized with their situation.

• What steps did you take to investigate the issue and gather relevant information?

• Any decisions or solutions you proposed or implemented to resolve the problem.

Sample Response (Actions): *"To address the client's concerns, I immediately scheduled a meeting with them to have a thorough discussion about their grievances. During the meeting, I actively listened to their feedback, acknowledged their frustrations, and* *empathized with their situation. It was important to make the client feel heard and valued.*

Following the meeting, I conducted a detailed review of the project, including all correspondence, timelines, and quality checks. This helped me identify areas where we had fallen short and why the client was dissatisfied. I then presented a clear plan of action to rectify the issues, which included additional quality checks, revising timelines, and improving communication."

Step 3: Highlight the Results. Conclude your response by discussing the outcomes and results of your efforts to address the dissatisfied customer's concerns. Describe how your approach led to their satisfaction and any additional steps taken to ensure their ongoing happiness.

Sample Response (Results): *"As a result of the actions I took, we were able to successfully address the client's concerns and significantly improve their satisfaction. The client appreciated our* *prompt response, willingness to rectify the issues, and commitment*

to ensuring a positive outcome.

We successfully delivered the revised project within the new

agreed-upon timeline, with improved quality. Throughout the

process, I maintained regular communication with the client to

provide updates and address any further concerns. This proactive

approach not only resolved the immediate issue but also

strengthened our client relationship, leading to continued

collaboration and additional projects "

Key Tips:

- Use the STAR method (Situation, Task, Action, Result) to structure your response.

- Emphasize your customer service skills, empathy, and problem-solving abilities.

- Be specific about the actions you took and the impact of your solution.

- Highlight the positive outcomes and the restoration of customer satisfaction.

12.3 Initiative and Problem-Solving:

Sample Question 1: Describe a time when you had to take on a project or task outside of your job description. How did you handle the additional responsibilities, and what was the outcome?

Step 1: Set the Scene. Start by providing context and background information about the situation where you had to take on additional responsibilities beyond your job description. Include the following details:

- The company or organization where this occurred.

- Your usual job responsibilities and role.

- The specific project or task that required you to step outside of your job description.

Sample Response (Situation): *"In my previous role as a Marketing Coordinator at XYZ Company, I was primarily responsible for creating marketing materials and assisting with campaign execution. However, we encountered a situation where a key team member had to take extended medical leave right before a critical marketing campaign was about to launch. This unexpected absence left a significant gap in our team, and it was clear that I needed to step in and take on additional responsibilities to ensure the campaign's success."*

Step 2: Describe Your Actions. Explain the specific actions you took to handle the additional responsibilities effectively. Highlight the strategies and steps you employed to meet the project's demands, even if they were outside your usual job scope. Include the following aspects:

• How did you assess the situation and identify the tasks that needed to be addressed?

- The skills or knowledge you had to acquire or develop to fulfill these new responsibilities.

- Any challenges you encountered and how you overcame them.

Sample Response (Actions): *"To address the situation, I first conducted a thorough assessment of the tasks that needed immediate attention to keep the campaign on track. This included coordinating with external vendors, managing the campaign timeline, and overseeing the budget.*

One significant aspect of this situation was managing the campaign's digital marketing efforts, which were not part of my usual responsibilities. To bridge this gap, I proactively upskilled by taking online courses on digital marketing and seeking guidance from colleagues with expertise in this area.

Despite the tight timeline and added pressure, I organized the team effectively, ensured seamless communication, and closely monitored progress. I also had to make quick decisions and adapt to unforeseen challenges to keep the campaign running smoothly."

Step 3: Highlight the Results. Conclude your response by discussing the outcomes and results of your efforts to handle the additional responsibilities. Describe how your actions contributed to the successful completion of the project or task and any positive impact it had on your team or organization.

Sample Response (Results): *"As a result of the actions I took, we were able to successfully launch the marketing campaign on schedule and within the budget. Despite the initial challenges, our team achieved exceptional results, surpassing our campaign targets for engagement and conversions.*

Furthermore, my ability to step up and take on these additional responsibilities during a crucial period was acknowledged by both my team and management. It reinforced the importance of adaptability and teamwork within our organization.

This experience not only enhanced my skills and knowledge but also demonstrated my commitment to the team's success and my ability to excel in unexpected situations."

Key Tips:

• Use the STAR method (Situation, Task, Action, Result) to structure your response.

• Emphasize your adaptability, problem-solving abilities, and proactive approach.

• Be specific about the actions you took and the impact of your contributions.

• Highlight the positive outcomes and how your willingness to go beyond your job description benefited the team or organization.

Sample Question 2: Can you provide an example of a project where you had to work with a diverse team or with individuals from different backgrounds? How did you promote inclusivity and collaboration?

Step 1: Set the Scene Start by providing context and background information about the project where you worked with a diverse team or individuals from different backgrounds. Include the following details:

- The organization or company where this project took place.

- The nature of the project and its objectives.

- The diverse team members or individuals you collaborated with.

Sample Response (Situation): *"In my previous role at ABC Company, I was part of a cross-functional project team tasked with launching a new product in international markets. The team consisted of members from various departments, including marketing, sales, product development, and customer support. What made our team particularly diverse was the fact that we had* *team members from different cultural backgrounds, each bringing*

unique perspectives and experiences to the project."

Step 2: Describe Your Actions. Explain the specific actions you took to promote inclusivity and collaboration within the diverse team. Highlight strategies and steps you employed to ensure that everyone's voices were heard and that the team worked harmoniously toward the project's goals. Include the following aspects:

• How you encouraged open communication and active listening within the team.

• Any initiatives or activities you organized to build rapport and trust among team members.

• Examples of how you addressed and resolved conflicts, if any, arose during the project.

Sample Response (Actions): *"To promote inclusivity and collaboration within the team, I initiated several actions. Firstly, I* organized regular team meetings where we encouraged open discussions and ensured that every team member had the opportunity to share their thoughts and ideas. I made it a point to actively listen to everyone's perspectives and acknowledge the value of their contributions.

Additionally, I organized team-building activities outside of work hours, such as cultural exchange events and social gatherings, where team members could get to know each other on a personal level. These activities helped build trust and camaraderie among team members.

During the project, we did encounter a few instances of differing opinions due to our diverse backgrounds. In such cases, I took a proactive approach by facilitating constructive discussions and finding common ground. I made sure that conflicts were addressed respectfully and resolved through compromise, with the project's objectives always in mind."

Step 3: Highlight the Results. Conclude your response by discussing the outcomes and results of your efforts to promote inclusivity and collaboration within the diverse team. Describe how your actions contributed to the success of the project and any positive impact it had on team dynamics or project outcomes.

Sample Response (Results): *"As a result of our collective efforts to promote inclusivity and collaboration, our diverse team not only successfully launched the new product in international markets but also exceeded our sales targets by a significant margin. The diverse perspectives and innovative ideas contributed to a more comprehensive marketing strategy that resonated with a wide range of audiences.*

Furthermore, our team became more cohesive and strengthened the bonds among team members. This collaborative spirit continued beyond the project as we actively sought opportunities to work together on future initiatives. The project's success was not just about achieving business objectives; it was also about fostering an inclusive and collaborative work culture within the

organization."

Key Tips:

• Use the STAR method (Situation, Task, Action, Result) to structure your response.

• Emphasize your ability to facilitate collaboration, resolve conflicts, and promote inclusivity.

• Provide specific examples of actions you took to illustrate your points.

• Highlight the positive outcomes and the impact of your efforts on project success and team dynamics.

Sample Question 3: Tell me about a moment when you faced a setback or failure at work. How did you react to it, and what steps did you take to overcome the challenge?

Step 1: Set the Scene Start by providing context and background information about the specific setback or failure you encountered at work. Include the following details:

- The company or organization where this situation occurred.

- The nature of the project, task, or situation where the setback or failure occurred.

- The specific challenges or obstacles that led to the setback.

Sample Response (Situation): *"In my previous role at XYZ Corporation, I was leading a cross-functional team responsible for launching a new product. The project had tight deadlines, and we were facing intense competition in the market. However, despite our initial efforts, we encountered a significant setback when a key supplier failed to deliver critical components on time, jeopardizing our project timeline and launch date."*

Step 2: Describe Your Actions. Explain the specific actions you took in response to the setback or failure. Highlight the strategies and steps you employed to address the challenges and work toward a solution. Include the following aspects:

- How did you initially react to the setback, and what was your emotional response?

- The steps you took to assess the situation, identify the root causes, and understand the implications.

- Any decisions or actions you initiated to mitigate the impact of the setback and get the project back on track.

Sample Response (Actions): *"When we first learned about the supplier's delay, it was a moment of frustration and disappointment for the entire team, including myself. However, I understood that dwelling on the setback wouldn't help us overcome it. I immediately called for a team meeting to assess the situation comprehensively.*

During the meeting, we discussed the root causes of the supplier's delay, including potential miscommunications and unforeseen challenges on their end. To address the issue, I reached out to the

supplier personally to understand their constraints and explore

possible solutions. Simultaneously, I worked with our internal team

to revise the project timeline, reallocating resources and adjusting

deadlines where possible to minimize the impact.

We also implemented contingency plans and identified alternative

suppliers to ensure a consistent supply of critical components in

case the issue persisted. Additionally, I communicated

transparently with our stakeholders, including upper management

and clients, about the setback, the actions we were taking, and the

revised timeline."

Step 3: Highlight the Results. Conclude your response by
discussing the outcomes and results of your efforts to overcome the
setback or failure. Describe how your actions led to a resolution,
what you learned from the experience, and any positive changes or
improvements that resulted from the challenge.

Sample Response (Results): *"As a result of our collective efforts, we were able to address the supplier's delay and get the project back on track. While we did experience a slight timeline adjustment, it was significantly less than initially anticipated. Our team's ability to adapt, problem-solve, and remain resilient during this setback showcased our commitment to delivering results even in challenging situations.*

Moreover, this experience taught us the importance of supplier diversification and enhanced our risk management processes. We implemented a more robust supplier evaluation system to prevent similar issues in the future. Additionally, the open and transparent communication with stakeholders strengthened our client relationships, as they appreciated our honesty and commitment to delivering quality products."

Key Tips:

• Use the STAR method (Situation, Task, Action, Result) to structure your response.

- Highlight your ability to remain composed and take decisive actions in response to setbacks.

- Emphasize what you learned from the experience and any positive changes that resulted.

- Show how your actions contributed to finding a solution and achieving the desired outcome.

12.4 Time Management and Multitasking:

- Share an experience where you had to multitask and manage multiple priorities simultaneously. How did you stay organized and ensure all tasks were completed efficiently?

Step 1: Set the Scene. Start by providing context and background information about the situation where you had to multitask and manage multiple priorities. Include the following details:

- The company or organization where this situation occurred.

- The specific project, role, or responsibilities that required multitasking.

- The various tasks or priorities that needed simultaneous management.

Sample Response (Situation): *"In my previous role as a project manager at ABC Company, I was responsible for overseeing multiple client projects simultaneously. These projects were diverse in scope, had different timelines, and involved various teams within the organization. As a project manager, my role was to ensure that each project progressed smoothly and met its respective deadlines."*

Step 2: Describe Your Actions. Explain the specific actions you took to manage multiple priorities and tasks effectively. Highlight the strategies and techniques you employed to stay organized, set priorities, and ensure that all tasks were completed efficiently. Include the following aspects:

- How did you assess the tasks and determine their relative importance and urgency?

236

- Any tools, systems, or methodologies you used to stay organized and track progress.

- Examples of effective time management and delegation, if applicable.

Sample Response (Actions): *"To manage multiple priorities, I began by conducting a thorough assessment of each project's requirements and deadlines. I used a project management software that allowed me to create detailed project plans, set milestones, and allocate resources efficiently. This helped me visualize the overall workload and dependencies.*

Next, I implemented a priority system that categorized tasks based on their urgency and impact on project timelines. High-priority tasks that directly influenced project milestones received my immediate attention, while lower-priority tasks were scheduled in a way that ensured their completion without jeopardizing critical deadlines.

Additionally, I practiced effective time management by allocating specific time blocks for focused work on each project. I minimized distractions during these blocks to maximize productivity. When feasible, I delegated certain tasks to team members, ensuring that everyone's strengths were leveraged to the fullest."

Step 3: Highlight the Results. Conclude your response by discussing the outcomes and results of your efforts to multitask and manage multiple priorities efficiently. Describe how your actions contributed to the successful completion of tasks and projects while maintaining quality and meeting deadlines.

Sample Response (Results): *"As a result of my approach to multitasking and priority management, our team consistently met project deadlines and delivered high-quality work. Clients commended our ability to maintain open communication and provide timely updates on project progress.*

Furthermore, our projects were completed within budget, and we experienced a significant reduction in missed deadlines and scope creep. By efficiently managing multiple priorities, we not only meet client expectations but also increase client satisfaction, leading to repeat business and referrals."

Key Tips:

• Use the STAR method (Situation, Task, Action, Result) to structure your response.

• Emphasize your ability to prioritize effectively and maintain organization.

• Showcase how your actions contributed to the successful completion of tasks and projects.

• Highlight any tools or systems you used to enhance your multitasking capabilities.